school success for kids with

ADHD

school success for kids with

ADHD

Stephan M. Silverman,
Jacqueline S. Iseman, and Sue Jeweler

PRUFROCK PRESS INC.

WACO, TEXAS

Library of Congress Cataloging-in-Publication Data

Silverman, Stephan M., 1942-
  School success for kids with ADHD / Stephan M. Silverman, Jacqueline S. Iseman, and Sue Jeweler.
    p. cm.
  Includes bibliographical references.
  ISBN-13: 978-1-59363-358-5 (pbk.)
  ISBN-10: 1-59363-358-0 (pbk.)
  1. Attention-deficit-disordered children—Education. 2. Attention-deficit hyperactivity disorder—Treatment. I. Iseman, Jacqueline S., 1977- II. Jeweler, Sue, 1947- III. Title.
  LC4713.2.S55 2009
  371.94—dc22
                    2008051481

Copyright © 2009 Prufrock Press Inc.
Edited by Lacy Compton
Cover and Layout Design by Marjorie Parker

ISBN-13: 978-1-59363-358-5
ISBN-10: 1-59363-358-0

Printed in the United States of America.

At the time of this book's publication, all facts and figures cited are the most current available. All telephone numbers, addresses, and Web site URLs are accurate and active. All publications, organizations, Web sites, and other resources exist as described in the book, and all have been verified. The authors and Prufrock Press Inc. make no warranty or guarantee concerning the information and materials given out by organizations or content found at Web sites, and we are not responsible for any changes that occur after this book's publication. If you find an error, please contact Prufrock Press Inc.

Prufrock Press Inc.
P.O. Box 8813
Waco, TX 76714-8813
Phone: (800) 998-2208
Fax: (800) 240-0333
http://www.prufrock.com

Dedication

To our parents, Milton and Judith Silverman, Sheila and Joseph Iseman, and Ruth and Mel Blaustein, who always modeled how to pay attention to the wonders in the world.

We also would like to dedicate this book to our families: Steve's wife, Karin Silverman, son Gabriel Silverman, and daughter, Shoshana Silverman Belisle, who contributed to this book. Jackie would like to thank her husband, Greg, for always supporting her and her passions and especially for his enthusiastic encouragement while writing this book. Sue thanks her husband, Larry, for his words of wisdom, guidance, and love, and her children, Brie and Tom, and granddaughter, Alexis.

This book also is dedicated to all of those who are challenged by ADHD and those who care for them and work to help them discover their strengths and gifts.

Contents

Acknowledgements

We would like to acknowledge those who have made wonderful contributions to the development of this book. They share their passion for youngsters, adolescents, and adults who struggle with ADHD, and are committed to providing the best practices to individuals so that they will become successful in school and beyond.

Our contributing authors shared their extensive knowledge and expertise to enrich this project. **Dr. Lance D. Clawson** is responsible for the content of Chapter 3: The Medical Perspective and made additional contributions throughout the book; **Shoshana Silverman Belisle** wrote Chapter 10: A Review of Alternative Treatments Parents Can Consider; and **Jennifer Engel Fisher** is responsible for the content of Chapter 7: The Power and Techniques of Effective Coaching and made contributions to other chapters as well. Shoshana would like to thank Dr. Benjamin Kliger for his review of her chapter.

We wish to acknowledge Lacy Elwood Compton, our Prufrock editor extraordinaire, for her vision, counsel, and leadership throughout this project.

Finally, to those who went before us in the field of ADHD research: Drs. Howard Abikoff, Russell Barkley, Francisco Xavier Castellanos, Keith Conners, George DuPaul, Michael Gordon, Sam Goldstein, Ross Greene, Lawrence Greenhill, Barbara Ingersoll, Peter Jenkins, Allan Mirsky, Kathleen Nadeau, Jack Naglieri, William Pelham, Thomas Phelan, David Rabiner, Cecil Reynolds, and Larry Silver and the scores of researchers who we may have failed to mention.

Introduction

JACK struggles in school, especially in completing assignments on time. Although his teachers frequently comment that he seems bright, they also note that he is distracted easily and that he often needs reminders to stay focused on his classwork. He is a daydreamer who talks with classmates at inappropriate times. Jack looks out the window or wanders around the classroom. He also gets in trouble for calling out while his teacher is presenting a lesson.

At home, Jack's behavior is quite similar. His parents note that he easily forgets what he is supposed to be doing and has trouble getting up in the morning and going to bed at night. He loses things like toys and games, gets in trouble for climbing on the couch, and can't sit still at the dinner table. Jack has difficulty making and keeping friends. His peers often complain that he interrupts them and won't take turns.

Jack's symptoms are typical of individuals with Attention Deficit Hyperactivity Disorder (ADHD).

Each year in the United States an estimated 184,450 youth are given the principal diagnosis of ADHD (Milazzo-Sayre et al., 2001). According to the text revision of the American Psychiatric Association's *Diagnostic and Statistical Manual of Mental Disorders, Fourth Edition* (DSM-IV-TR; APA, 2000) a handbook for listing different categories of mental disorders and the criteria for diagnosing them, individuals with ADHD constitute 3%–5% of the school-aged population. Therefore, in a class of 25 to 30 children, it is likely that at least one student will have this condition. Given the widespread occurrence of attention problems, it is important for society to have an understanding of this disorder and how to best support children and adolescents with attention deficits.

School Success for Kids With ADHD is written for parents, educators, and other professionals working with children. It presents a dynamic, comprehensive, practical, and effective approach to address the needs of a child or adolescent like Jack. Specific, concrete, and research-based strategies are presented for helping individuals with ADHD in a school setting from preschool through college and beyond.

This book includes an explanation of how ADHD is clearly differentiated from a variety of other attention problems; a look at depression, anxiety, and other learning issues that appear similar to ADHD; major important historical and current research initiatives; cutting-edge pharmaceutical interventions and other medically relevant findings by a noted child and adolescent psychiatrist; strategies parents can implement to help a child with attention deficits; a practical guide for coaching individuals with executive functioning issues (self-directed action); a research-based review of alternative treatments; best practices in the classroom; an evaluation of the popular myths surrounding ADHD; and an emphasis on research-based truths about etiology and presentation of symptoms. This book includes a list of resources on the disorder in the Resources section.

The power of *School Success for Kids With ADHD* lies in recognizing the importance of teamwork to effectively treat individuals with attention deficits. Therefore, the book contains a 12-point action plan for teachers and parents working together in a collaboration of stakeholders, including the child, which is found in Chapter 5. The other chapters cover a variety of issues of pertinence to parents and educators of students with ADHD.

Throughout history, many who struggled with ADHD have made significant contributions to society. Famous scientists, writers, artists, inventors, athletes, industrialists, and entertainers with the disorder have become successful individuals who are role models to others. Their personal vision and resilience, along with the support of their parents, teachers, and mentors, empowered them to great heights of achievement. A list of these individuals can be found in Appendix A, along with other tools that can be used with individuals with ADHD. We urge you to share this list with children and adolescents with attention problems as a source of encouragement and guidance. Explanations on how you can use the other tools in Appendix A are scattered throughout the following chapters.

Understanding the scientific and medical research behind any disorder is a must for parents and professionals working with this population. Thus, Appendix B offers an extensive overview of the current research taking place regarding ADHD, along with information on recent research studies that have affected how professionals perceive, recognize, and work with this disorder. In particular, a section on the diagnosis of ADHD has been included to assist parents and professionals in understanding the diagnostic process for determining whether an individual has ADHD.

We hope that this book will provide you with the necessary information and tools you need for supporting your own child, or the children with whom you work each day, in school and beyond!

chapter 1

The Importance and Impact of Attention

"If I put my mind to it I can do just about anything."

Michael Phelps, Olympic champion
and record holder

NOTHING of value can be accomplished without focus and concentration. The power of concentration characterizes those who truly excel in any field. Achievement requires the ability to sustain attention, to sacrifice other impulses, to resist distraction, to postpone pleasures, and to act with timing and judgment. These qualities separate those who are great in any field from others.

As the authors created this book, an unprecedented event took place in Beijing, China. Michael Phelps, the phenomenal young swimmer, shattered the record number of gold medals earned in a single sport at an Olympic games. According to the media, his was the "greatest individual triumph in Olympic history" (Jenkins, 2008). Michael's inspirational story reflects the athlete's commitment to achieving his personal best and also his deep understanding of the meaning of sportsmanship and humility. The impact of his accomplishment is heightened by the fact that he has ADHD and frequently was in trouble for disruptive behavior in the pool and at school.

His mom, a teacher, school administrator, and his greatest advocate, explained that he never sat still, never stopped talking, never stopped asking questions, and had difficulty staying on task. One of Michael's elementary school teachers said to her that Michael was unable to focus on anything. However, Mrs. Phelps knew that her son had exceptional focus when swimming. His ability to "hyperfocus" on his goals contributed to his success as a swimmer. In his own words, Michael said, "If I put my mind to it I can do just about anything" (Low, 2008).

Michael's story is repeated daily by children, adolescents, and adults with ADHD. They may not be Olympic stars, but with appropriate and effective support, guidance, and treatment by parents, educators, and other professionals working together as a team, these individuals with attention deficits can find resounding success and make exceptional contributions to the world.

Michael does not stand alone in his ability to "hyperfocus" on his goals. It is said that Sir Isaac Newton once worked on some theories sitting under a tree. A brass band went by him while he worked. A passerby interrupted Newton's studies and asked in which direction the band was traveling. Newton could not answer the question, because he didn't notice the band, let alone what direction it was going in. He was too absorbed in his studies. With practice, great meditators can continue to concentrate in loud environments, even when construction is going on, for example. Disciples of spiritual masters are known to sit in silence for hours with single-pointed attention.

Being poised "at the ready" to focus is a prelude to many activities, whether it is practicing martial arts, standing at attention in military exercises, waiting for a pitch in baseball, holding a linebacker's lunge in football, preparing for the first note of a symphony, or awaiting a cue to go on stage. In some cultures, such as in parts of India, for example, children are taught to sit with their legs crossed in a straight posture while awaiting the arrival of their teacher in the classroom for the day's lessons. They are "primed" to attend. This is not to say that there are no children who have trouble with such discipline in India. Children with difficulties in attention and restraint are born into every culture. In every culture, however, most productive activities require the ability to maintain focus. Schooling is a universal experience in human development where attention is required to access its content and skills. These abilities, the aggregate of skills that make up sustained attention and restraint, are of great importance in life in and out of school.

The goal of every life is crowned by self-knowledge and the discovery of strengths. When these strengths are combined with passion, a personal mission, then the power of attention can be focused and enabled. It is our hope that every child, especially those with challenges in attending and restraining action, can be recognized for their strengths and that the power of self-knowledge and passion can be harnessed and focused for their own fulfillment.

The more information we know and understand about ADHD and its impact on individuals, the better able we are to create a thoughtful, collaborative, and effective approach that successfully addresses the strengths and needs of those who deal with attention challenges every day.

What is Attention Deficit Hyperactivity Disorder and why must we be concerned about its impact on children?

Attention Deficit Hyperactivity Disorder (ADHD) is a mental disorder of childhood characterized by symptoms of inattention, hyperactivity, and impulsivity. In order to be diagnosed, these symptoms must occur more frequently and be more serious than those normally observed in individuals with a similar level of development. Additionally, in order to accurately clinically distinguish ADHD from other diagnoses, the symptoms must be present in two or more contexts, must appear before the age of 7, and must cause a clinically significant deterioration of social, academic, or work-related activities.

Despite the amount of press ADHD has received, individuals with ADHD only constitute approximately 3%–5% of the school-aged population (American Psychiatric Association, 2000). According to a Client/Patient Sample Survey collected by the Center for Mental Health Services in 1997, which provided detailed information about the status of youth and adults in mental health care, individuals with ADHD represent the largest group referred for services (Milazzo-Sayre et al., 2001). Clinical experience bears this out in daily practice. These individuals comprised 14% of the total youth population admitted for services each year (Milazzo-Sayre et al., 2001). Due to the high prevalence rate of ADHD among youth, as well as the frequent utilization of health services by this population, ADHD is a considerable public health issue (Scahill et al., 1999).

Causes of ADHD

Although no one is exactly sure what factors cause ADHD, research suggests that there is a combination of causes, including genetics and environmental influences. Although several factors could increase an individual's likelihood of having ADHD, physical differences in the brain seem to be involved (see Chapter 3 for an in-depth discussion).

Family History

Although the precise causes of ADHD have yet to be identified, there is little question that biological contributions are the largest factor in the expression of this disorder (Barkley & Murphy, 2006). It is estimated that the likelihood of inheriting ADHD is about 80%, which means that genetic factors account for approximately 80% of the differences among individuals with this set of behavioral symptoms. According to the American Academy of Child & Adolescent Psychiatry (AACAP; 2008), more than one-third of fathers who had ADHD during their own childhood had a child who met the criteria for ADHD.

Prenatal and Perinatal Risks

In instances where heredity does not seem to play a role, difficulties during pregnancy, as well as prenatal exposure to alcohol and tobacco, appear to contribute to the risk for this disorder. Additionally, premature delivery, significantly low birth weights, and postnatal injury to the prefrontal regions of the brain all contribute to the risk for ADHD in varying degrees (Barkley & Murphy, 2006). We also cannot disregard many of the abnormalities of delivery and early development including a wrapped cord, a "blue baby," a seizure, high temperatures, or any cause of oxygen loss or chemical insult to the developing brain.

Environmental Toxins

It has been found that children who are exposed to very high levels of lead before 6 years of age also might be at a higher risk for ADHD. Young children may become exposed to lead when they spend time in older buildings with a build-up of dust from chipped paint that contains lead or from drinking water that was delivered through lead pipes (AACAP, 2008).

The Subtypes of ADHD

The text revision of the DSM-IV-TR (APA, 2000) identifies three types of ADHD including the predominantly inattentive type, the predominantly hyperactive/impulsive type, and the combined type, in which an individual displays both inattentive and hyperactive/impulsive symptoms. A reprinting of the DSM criteria for ADHD is included in Figure 1.

The Inattentive Child

Children diagnosed with the predominantly inattentive type of ADHD may get bored with an activity quickly, particularly if the task

Inattentive type:

    Six or more of the following symptoms of inattention have persisted for at least 6 months to a degree that is maladaptive and inconsistent with developmental level:

1. Often fails to give close attention to details or makes careless mistakes in schoolwork, work, or other activities
2. Often has difficulty sustaining attention in tasks or play activities
3. Often does not seem to listen when spoken to directly
4. Often does not follow through on instructions and fails to finish schoolwork, chores, or duties in the workplace (not due to oppositional behavior or failure to understand instructions)
5. Often has difficulty organizing tasks and activities
6. Often avoids, dislikes, or is reluctant to engage in tasks that require sustained mental effort (such as school work or homework)
7. Often loses things necessary for tasks or activities (e.g., toys, school assignments, pencils, books, or tools)
8. Is often easily distracted by extraneous stimuli
9. Is often forgetful in daily activities

Hyperactive/Impulsive type:

    Six or more of the following symptoms of hyperactivity/impulsivity have persisted for at least 6 months to a degree that is maladaptive and inconsistent with developmental level

Hyperactivity

1. Often fidgets with hands or feet or squirms in seat
2. Often leaves seat in classroom or in other situations in which remaining seated is expected
3. Often runs about or climbs excessively in situations in which it is inappropriate (in adolescents or adults, may be limited to subjective feelings of restlessness)
4. Often has difficulty playing or engaging in leisure activities quietly
5. Is often "on the go" or often acts as if "driven by a motor"
6. Often talks excessively

Impulsivity

1. Often blurts out answers before questions have been completed
2. Often has difficulty awaiting turn
3. Often interrupts or intrudes on others (e.g. butts into conversations or games)

Figure 1. **DSM-IV-TR criteria.**

is not one that they enjoy. They struggle with organization and planning a task in order to be able to complete it or to learn something new. As students, children with the inattentive type of ADHD frequently have difficulty remembering to copy down school assignments and to bring home books and other school materials. Additionally, completing homework can be a very large challenge. Often they are thought to have a memory problem, when, in fact, they missed "registering" information in the first place.

Throughout life, individuals with the inattentive type of ADHD are easily distracted and may make many careless mistakes in their academics, work, or personal lives. They frequently are forgetful, have difficulty following instructions, and skip from one activity to another without finishing the first activity.

It is extremely important to note that an inattentive child with ADHD often may be able to sit quietly in class and appear to be working. However, frequently this student is not really focusing on the assignment. Therefore, it is common for teachers and parents to overlook the problem.

The Hyperactive/Impulsive Child

Children with the predominantly hyperactive/impulsive type of ADHD always seem to be in motion. They may move around, touch or play with whatever is nearby, or talk unremittingly. In school, during story time or instruction, these children may squirm around in their seats, fidget, or get up and move about the classroom. These children frequently wiggle or tap their feet and fingers. They may blurt out comments or answers without thinking first. Frequently, they also may display their emotions without restraint or forget to consider the consequences of their actions. Hyperactive/impulsive children typically find it difficult to wait in line or take turns.

A teenager or adult who is hyperactive/impulsive may describe feeling restless or a need to stay busy all of the time. These teenagers and adults tend to make choices based on their small immediate payoff rather than persistently working toward a larger delayed reward. In general, children with these symptoms come across as being impatient. They may only get part of a communication because they stop listening before the speaker is finished.

Coexisting Disorders and Their Frequencies in Childhood

ADHD, in and of itself, is a challenge, but what often separates straightforward instances from those that are very challenging to manage are those with ADHD who also suffer from a variety of frequently associated neuropsychiatric disorders. The frequently occurring additional diagnoses are described as *comorbidities*. According to the National Institute of Mental Health (NIMH; 2008c), there are several disorders that sometimes accompany childhood ADHD. The following disorders are most frequently found as coexisting disorders with ADHD in childhood.

Learning Disabilities, Language Difficulties, and Areas of Cognitive Weakness

Learning disabilities are the most common comorbidity seen with ADHD. Between 24% and 70% of all individuals with ADHD are believed to suffer from some type of learning problem (Barkley, 2006; however, it must be kept in mind that studies differ, as do the ways learning disabilities are defined). According to NIMH (2008c), approximately 20%–30% of children with ADHD also have a diagnosable, specific learning disability (LD). During the preschool years, these disabilities can appear as difficulties in understanding certain sounds or words, as well as difficulty in expressing oneself verbally. During the school age years, reading or spelling disabilities, writing disorders, and arithmetic disorders are common among children with ADHD. Reading disabilities (dyslexia) are seen in 8%–39% of individuals with ADHD, while spelling difficulties are seen in 12%–30% of cases. Dyscalculia (a mathematics learning difficulty) is observed 12%–27% of the time, and handwriting difficulties (dysgraphia) are present in more than 60% of children with ADHD (Barkley, 2006). Thus, any child with ADHD should be carefully screened for associated learning problems.

Another complex aspect of ADHD is that even without a formal reading or language disorder, reading and listening comprehension deficits still are observed frequently, due to the limitations seen in working memory that frequently accompanies ADHD. (Working memory is explained simply by how much you can hold in your mind at one time, like the RAM on a computer; see p. 26.)

Language disorders, often associated with other learning problems, are diagnosed often. Expressive language deficits are seen in 10%–54% of individuals, and "pragmatic language" problems are noted 60% of the time (language pragmatics are loosely defined as language usage for the purpose of social interaction/dialogue; Barkley, 2006). Children with ADHD and associated language problems often display excessive speech, reduced fluency, and overall speech that is less logical, coherent, and organized.

The difficulty with working memory noted above, and other associated issues with language processing, often results in children with ADHD demonstrating a delayed internalization of language or internal self-talk. This is linked to what often is described as a reduced capacity for rule-governed behavior in individuals with ADHD. It's more difficult for them to "talk themselves through" any given experience; thus they can be less self-observing and less mindful of themselves.

Lower Average Intelligence (7–10 point deficit) in IQ testing is generally seen in children with ADHD as a group. This discrepancy is felt to be due to an apparent failure to keep pace with peers academically because of the overall impact of ADHD, but also could result from poor executive functioning (see p. 23) that partly affects IQ testing results.

Motor and Other Physical Symptoms

Motor symptoms are another common accompanying issue in children with ADHD. These symptoms have been described as *dys-*

praxia (motor planning), where a significant population of children with ADHD will have difficulty executing both fine and/or gross motor tasks such as writing, buttoning buttons or snapping snaps, tying shoelaces, or throwing and catching a ball. Occupational therapists and psychologists measure many of these same capacities and describe them as *visual-motor integration* abilities. In addition to having many of the motor planning issues above, children with visual-motor integration difficulties also have trouble copying complex designs and representing what they are thinking and seeing on the page. Formal diagnoses of these visual-motor and fine motor problems are termed a *developmental coordination disorder*. More than 50% of children with ADHD qualify for this diagnosis (Barkley, 2006). As a group, and linked to many of the motor issues noted above, children with ADHD show reduced physical fitness, strength, and stamina.

When children are diagnosed with a seizure disorder, their chance of also having ADHD is 2.5 more likely (approximately 20% of children with seizures also have ADHD; Barkley, 2006). In addition, sleep disorders occur in 30%–56% of children with ADHD, and the majority are mainly bedtime behavior problems, in that children with ADHD often have difficulty settling down and going to sleep without a set bedtime routine and good sleep hygiene practiced within the home. The more pronounced of these sleep initiation problems are diagnosable as delayed sleep onset disorder. Even while asleep, children with ADHD move four times more frequently than peers without ADHD (they are hyperactive even while unconscious!). Additionally, many children with ADHD have shorter overall sleep times due to waking up frequently in the night. This shorter sleep time may exacerbate attention problems in school as well. Two important sleep disorders to consider when a child with ADHD has significant problems with sleep are sleep apnea and restless leg syndrome (discussed in Chapter 3).

Barkley (2006) notes that motor tic disorders are seen in 10%–15% of children with ADHD, with peak onset between the ages of 8 to 10 years of age. Tourette syndrome (motor and vocal tics) is relatively rare, occurring in only 2% of children with ADHD (Barkley, 2000). However, 50%–80% of children diagnosed with Tourette syndrome also will suffer from ADHD (Barkley; this is what is termed a *one-way comorbidity*). Tourette syndrome is named for Georges Gilles de la Tourette, who first described this disorder in 1885 (Robertson, 2000). People with Tourette syndrome frequently have various nervous tics and repetitive mannerisms, including eye blinks, facial twitches, or grimacing. Other individuals with Tourette syndrome may clear their throats frequently, snort, sniff, or bark out words. However, these behaviors often can be controlled with medication.

Anxiety and Mood Disorders

Anxiety disorders co-occur with ADHD in 10%–40% of cases (Barkley, 2006). Interestingly, if only parents are interviewed about the presence or absence of anxiety in their child with ADHD, the diagnosis often is missed, as anxiety symptoms often can be very private and have not been revealed. Anxiety in individuals with ADHD may be related in part to the poor emotion regulation that we commonly see in ADHD. Although legitimate anxiety disorders are likely, the most common are simple phobias or separation anxiety in early childhood. Generalized anxiety disorder becomes more common with age, and these individuals often show lower levels of impulsiveness when compared to their nonanxious peers. In children with ADHD (as well as children without ADHD), we also see that anxiety disorders are more likely to be present in their parents and other family members. In the clinical setting, it often is observed that comorbid cases are more impaired than pure ADHD cases. If the symptoms of anxiety are recognized and treated, the child likely will be more equipped to manage the problems that accompany his or her ADHD. Additionally, when a child with these coexisting disorders receives effective treatment for ADHD it can have a positive impact on his or her anxiety, as the child will be better able to successfully complete academic tasks.

Obsessive-compulsive disorder (OCD), an anxiety disorder, is relatively rare in individuals with ADHD and seen in 3%–4% of adults with ADHD, according to Barkley (2006). OCD is common in Tourette syndrome and seen in up to 30% of individuals with the syndrome (Barkley, 2006). OCD behavior is more likely (11%) in children with ADHD and is associated with lower family history of ADHD, better attention at school, perfectionism and possibly greater inhibition and OCD tendencies at home (Barkley, 2006).

Depression likely has some sort of genetic linkage to ADHD, as it appears thus far that the genetic coding for ADHD creates a vulnerability to major depressive disorder (MDD). Barkley (2006) noted that individuals with ADHD are about three times as likely to suffer a depressive disorder compared to their peers. MDD often is expressed upon exposure to repeated social and emotional distress, physical trauma, and other adverse life events. Many individuals with ADHD prone to developing MDD initially manifest low self-esteem in childhood, whereas the full syndrome of depression may not be fully apparent until adolescence or later. Individuals with both ADHD and MDD are at a greater risk for self-harm compared to those with MDD alone. They experience suicidal ideas four times as often and make suicide attempts twice as often (Barkley, 2006). Compared to their depressed (but non-ADHD) peers, depressed teens with ADHD acknowledge suicidal ideation while in high school (33% vs. 22%), and make more suicide attempts during high school (16% vs. 3%; Barkley, 2006). Their attempts are generally more serious with 46% (compared to 11% of non-ADHD peers) being psychiatrically hospitalized (Barkley, 2006). As adults, depressed individuals with ADHD generally show twice the rate of suicidal ideation and suicide attempts compared to those who are depressed without suffering from ADHD (Barkley, 2006).

The co-occurence of both ADHD and bipolar disorder (BPD) is well known, but there has been controversy as to the actual frequency. Part of this struggle may arise from the fact that differentiating between ADHD and bipolar disorder in childhood can be quite challenging. Bipolar disorder is classically characterized by moods cycling between periods of intense highs and lows. However, in children, bipolar disorder often appears as rather chronic mood dysregulation, with a mixture of elation, depression, and irritability. Furthermore, some symptoms can be present both in ADHD and bipolar disorder. These overlapping symptoms include a high level of energy and a reduced need for sleep.

Co-occurrence rates have been reported to vary, with up to 27% of children with ADHD suffering from BPD (Barkley, 2006). It seems that the higher rates are perhaps due to studies that may have over-diagnosed BPD in irritable, poorly regulated children with ADHD who appeared quite impaired at the time of diagnosis, but there wasn't sufficient follow-up to warrant making a diagnosis of BPD. Current consensus cites the incidence of BPD in all individuals with ADHD to be between 3% and 6% (Barkley, 2006). Although teasing out the two diagnoses can be challenging, individuals rarely display some of the cardinal signs of BPD such as grandiosity, hypersexuality, and disturbed thinking, as well as actual mania. On the other hand, there may be a one-way cormobidity (like we see in Tourette syndrome) where it has been shown that once diagnosed with BPD, there is an 80%–97% chance that the child also suffers from ADHD (E. Leibenluft, M.D., personal communication, Oct 2007).

Substance Abuse

Substance abuse is a serious public health concern and a frequent comorbid condition with ADHD. Alcohol and drug abuse occur in 10%–24% of individuals with ADHD (approximately 2 to 2.5 times more often than the non-ADHD population; Barkley, 2006). There is greater use of alcohol, tobacco, and marijuana, but hard drug use is related mostly to comorbid conduct disorder (see next section). It appears that substance abuse is closely tied to peer relationships with other substance-abusing peers.

Oppositional Defiant and Conduct Disorder

Oppositional defiant disorder (ODD) is present in 40%–80% of children with ADHD (Barkley, 2006). ODD mostly affects boys, and those with the disorder often are defiant, stubborn, and noncompliant. Children with ODD frequently have temper outbursts and become belligerent. Arguing with adults and refusing to obey also is common among these children. The neurological underpinnings of attention deficits contribute to and likely cause ODD through the impact of ADHD on emotional self-regulation (an executive function), and appear to account for the well-established findings that medications reduce ODD as much as they do ADHD symptoms. Another facet of the ODD phenomenon is related to disrupted parenting. Inconsistent, indiscriminate, emotional, and episodically harsh and permissive (lax) consequences are causally connected to the development of ODD. These types of poor parenting can arise from parental ADHD, as well as other high-risk parental disorders in families. Unfortunately, early onset ODD predicts persistence of ADHD over the lifespan.

Approximately 20%–40% of children with ADHD may eventually develop conduct disorder (CD; NIMH, 2008c). CD is thought to be an outgrowth in some children with ODD. It is a condition manifested by a persistent pattern of rule breaking and antisocial behavior and is comorbid 20%–56% of the time (Barkley, 2006). Psychopathy is seen in 20% of individuals with ADHD (Barkley, 2006). These individuals display more severe and more persistent antisocial behavior. When there is poorer family psychopathology and antisocial personality, substance abuse and MDD are common co-occurring disorders with conduct disorder. These individuals are less responsive to treatment than late onset (older than age 12) cases, and are at high risk for lifelong criminal behavior. If the symptoms begin later in adolescence, it appears to be more related to social disadvantage, family disruption, and deviant peers. Father desertion and parental divorce also appear to affect MDD, school dropout, and teen pregnancy. In general, children with ADHD are more than twice as likely to be arrested as compared to their same aged peers (Barkley, 2006). The behaviors frequently associated with conduct disorder involve:

- frequently lying or stealing;
- fighting with or bullying others;
- getting into trouble at school or with the police;
- violating the basic rights of other people;
- acting aggressively toward people or animals;

- destroying property, breaking into people's homes, committing thefts, carrying or using weapons, or engaging in vandalism; and

- experimenting with substance use, and later dependence on and abuse of substances.

When a clinician is evaluating an individual it is important that he or she attempts to determine whether one "primary" condition can fully account for the most disabling and distressing symptoms experienced by the individual (Faraone & Kunwar, 2007). If a primary condition can fully explain all of these symptoms, then another condition should not be diagnosed. For example, if a patient has ADHD-like symptoms that only occur during episodes of bipolarity, ADHD would not be diagnosed. In practice, it is frequently difficult to determine which symptoms are causing the patient's impairments, particularly when both disorders have a chronic course. However, if both conditions contribute to the patient's impairments, then both ADHD and the coexisting condition should be diagnosed and treated.

What Is Not ADHD?

Most individuals are easily distracted or have trouble finishing tasks at one time or another. However, to receive a diagnosis of ADHD, the behaviors must appear before 7 years of age and continue consistently for a period of at least 6 months. The symptoms also must cause limitations in functioning in at least two areas of the individual's life.

For children, these difficulties may appear in the classroom, in the home, in the community, or in social settings. If a child seems to experience symptoms in just one setting, such as on the playground, but not in other situations, such as with her family, the problem might represent an issue other than ADHD. Many other conditions and life issues can trigger symptoms that resemble ADHD. For example, a child may exhibit behaviors that mimic the symptoms when he experiences a sudden change in his personal life such as a death or divorce in the family (see below). This child simply may be preoccupied. Additionally, when children have problems with schoolwork caused by a learning disability or by anxiety or depression, the symptoms can resemble ADHD. Sometimes children have experienced a family conflict or trauma, or even punishment, which results in a high activity level as an escape from internal distress. This may really be an "agitated depression." It frequently is observed that children who have experienced abuse (including sexual abuse) may cope with their suffering through an automatic dissociation. They may seem to be "spaced out." Other neurological conditions (covered in Chapter 3) may appear to be similar to attention deficits. Therefore, it is essential to examine other possible reasons for the child's symptoms without jumping to the conclusion that they represent ADHD.

Other Conditions That Resemble ADHD

There are many other life situations and conditions that may resemble ADHD. When making the diagnosis of ADHD, a professional's first responsibility is to gather enough information to rule out other possible reasons for the child's behavior. Among other possible causes for symptoms similar to ADHD are the following:

- a sudden change in the child's life including the death of a close family member, such as a parent or grandparent; parents' divorce; or a parent's loss of his or her job;

- undetected seizures in the child, such as petit mal or temporal lobe seizures;

- a middle ear infection suffered by the child that causes intermittent hearing problems;

- other medical disorders that the child has that may affect brain functioning;

- underachievement in the child caused by learning disability; and
- childhood anxiety or depression.

In ruling out other potential causes for the ADHD-like symptoms, the NIMH (2008b) emphasizes that it is important for professionals to examine the child's school and medical records when making a diagnosis. The professional should check the school record for any evidence of hearing or vision problems, because most schools automatically screen for these. It also is crucial for the professional to analyze the home and classroom environments to determine if they are unusually stressful or chaotic and, similarly, how the child's parents and teachers interact with the child to recognize any other possible reasons for the ADHD-like behaviors, such as abuse or neglect.

Gender

Although girls can be diagnosed with ADHD, interestingly, boys are at a much higher risk with approximately 2 to 3 times more boys than girls having the diagnosis of ADHD (American Academy of Child & Adolescent Psychiatry, 2008). Girls with ADHD are more likely than boys to have the predominantly inattentive type of ADHD. They also are less likely to have a learning disability or to have problems in school or in their recreational time (Biederman et al., 2002). Biederman et al. (2002) also stated that girls are less likely to be identified and referred for assessment or treatment of ADHD because they are less likely to exhibit overt disruptive behaviors or aggression. Thus, it is likely that some girls with ADHD are overlooked. In general, boys tend to initially display greater impulsivity and motor restlessness to teachers, than those whose ADHD is primarily inattentive (often girls) and who seem to be sitting quietly and compliantly.

Impact of ADHD on a Daily Basis

ADHD often is described as a pervasive disorder because of the impact it has on multiple domains of functioning, including academics, peer relationships, family relationships, and self-esteem (Hazelwood, Bovingdon, & Tiemens, 2002). Children with ADHD have various special needs that impact most domains in their lives. These children are at risk for developing deficits in cognitive, social, family, and school functioning. Impairments in psychosocial domains and functioning within the home environment are common, as are difficulties in adjustment, social functioning, and internalizing and externalizing behavior (Barkley, 1990; Biederman et al., 1996).

ADHD also impacts a child's overall sustained effort and motivation. Barkley (1990) indicated that children with ADHD have poor sustained attention and have difficulty persisting with effort on tasks, particularly when they perceive the task as boring, tedious, or repetitive. Children with attention deficits frequently display a decreased level of persistence, "stick-to-it-tiveness," motivation, and willpower than their peers when given uninteresting yet important tasks. They often report becoming bored easily, causing them to shift from one uncompleted activity to another.

Research suggests that children with ADHD are at a greater risk for physical injuries, as well as accidental poisonings. Rowe, Maughan, and Goodman (2004) found a greater risk for fractures among children with attention problems, most likely due to their hyperactive and impulsive behavior. Additionally, children with ADHD are more likely than their peers to be injured as pedestrians, inflict injuries to themselves, sustain injuries to multiple regions of their bodies, and suffer head injuries (DiScala, Lescohier, Barthel, & Li, 1998). Interestingly, knowledge about safety does not seem to be lower in these children in comparison with their peers. Therefore, it is unlikely that interventions focused on increasing knowledge about safety would be effective (Mori & Peterson, 1995). In adolescence and adulthood, there are great risks attached to thrill-seeking and risk-taking associated with persons with ADHD.

Day-to-Day Inconsistencies

Individuals with ADHD experience greater than normal variability in their task or work performance (Barkley & Murphy, 2006). These inconsistencies especially are apparent among those subtypes associated with impulsive behavior. People with the hyperactive/impulsive type of ADHD commonly show substantial variability across time in the performance of their work. These wide swings may be found in the quality, quantity, and even speed of the work they produce. They frequently fail to maintain a relatively even pattern of productivity and accuracy in their work from moment to moment and day to day. This variability often is puzzling to teachers and parents who witness it. Educators and parents can be confused, as children with ADHD will sometimes complete their work quickly and correctly, while at others times perform tasks poorly, inaccurately, and quite erratically. Some researchers see this pattern of high variability in work-related activities to be a hallmark of the disorder.

Executive Functions

The most prevalent clinical view of ADHD maintains that the central deficits of the disorder are the inability to sustain attention and symptoms of hyperactivity and impulsivity. Over the past two decades, tremendous progress has been made in understanding the functions of the prefrontal cortex, which are believed to primarily include attention and control processes. This area of the brain is roughly highlighted in Figure 2.

These mental activities are unified under the term *executive functions* (EF). Anderson (1998) refers to EF as encompassing the skills necessary for purposeful, goal-directed activity. But, sometimes the definition is so broad that there is no clear area of the brain for all of the functions thought to encompass these abilities. Clearly, many areas of the brain work in concert in any behavior or behavioral sequence, while the prefrontal lobes may be critical in EF.

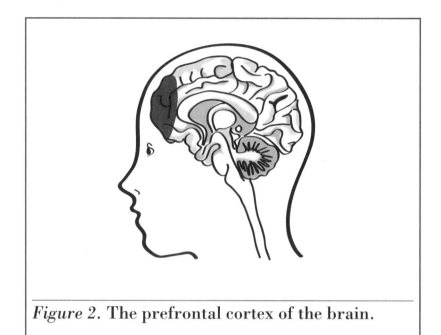

Figure 2. The prefrontal cortex of the brain.

Karl Pribram (1976) may have been the first to describe the executive functions of the prefrontal cortex functions necessary to maintain brain organization. Muriel Lezak defined EF as "those capacities that enable a person to engage successfully in independent, purposive, self-serving behavior" (Lezak, 1995, p. 42). The operational definition of what is contained in the concept of EF is still unclear and varies from one researcher to another. Barkley (2000a) uses the term to incorporate:

- volition, planning, and purposive, goal-directed, or intentional action;

- inhibition and resistance to distraction;

- problem solving and strategy development, selection, and monitoring;

- flexible shifting of actions to meet task demands;

- maintenance of persistence toward attaining a goal; and

- self-awareness across time.

Many authors have recognized the substantial overlap or inter-changeability between EF and self-regulation and the attention system. Some writers have thought of EF as regulated social action or social planning. Others have simply thrown up their hands at the lack of definition and declared EF to be what the frontal lobes of the brain do.

One function that is thought to be part of EF and is related to ADHD is response inhibition. Inhibition is involved when working memory (see below) is activated and must be resistant to interruption and interference.

Russell Barkley (2005) wrote a history of a model of EF in the revised edition of his book *ADHD and the Nature of Self-Control*. This model provided that cerebral regions are relatively immature during childhood, with development thought to be a protracted process, which continues into adolescence. Barkley describes this progression as follows:

- from external events to mental representations related to those events;

- from control by others to control by the self;

- from immediate reinforcement to delayed gratification; and

- from the now to the conjectured social future.

Barkley (2005) viewed self-regulation (SR) to be an inherent part of EF, making EF inherently future-directed, which involves response inhibition in goal-directed behavior. Response inhibition is the capacity to delay a response to an immediate environmental event. Response inhibition also permits the internalization or "privatization" of each EF. It does so by suppressing action. In the course of development, behavior becomes covert or mental in form. We talk ourselves into restraining from saying the wrong thing at the wrong time, for example.

Barkley (1997b) stated that in order to better understand the true nature of ADHD, we should go beyond the definition of the disorder that is presented in the DSM-IV-TR. He explained that ADHD involves a deficiency in behavioral inhibition. Behavioral inhibition requires refraining from an initial response to an immediate event in order to permit oneself a protected period of delay in which the executive functions of self-directed action may occur. In other words, behavioral inhibition involves the ability to stop and think before acting. This deficiency in behavioral inhibition is linked to impairments in four neuropsychological (executive) functions:

- working memory,

- self-regulation of affect-motivational-arousal,

- internalization of speech, and

- reconstitution.

Many researchers include working memory (WM) in the definition of EF. This is the capacity to hold a mental representation in mind to guide behavior. Sometimes WM is used to mean remembering for very short periods of time (shorter than short-term memory) as in trying to hold a phone number in mind while looking for a pencil. Usually, the working memory of a child is able to retain goals and intentions. Whereas short-term memory generally refers to the short-term storage of information, working memory also refers to structures and processes used for temporarily storing and manipulating information. Working memory allows a child to formulate and use action plans to guide performance of goal-directed responses. As such, working memory also can be thought of as working attention. However, because the behavioral inhibition is deficient among individuals with ADHD, their critical response delay is impaired. The child with ADHD typically does not have time to access working memory by stopping and thinking before acting. Therefore, she is not protected from the various sources of interference that may disrupt her processing.

Given that working memory is impaired among individuals with ADHD, their capacity to hold information in mind that will be used to guide one's actions, either at the moment or at a later time, is impaired. Working memory is essential for remembering to do things in the near future. Because individuals with ADHD often have difficulties with working memory, they are forgetful, unable to keep important information in mind that they will need to guide their actions later (such as remembering a phone number or even a short string of numbers or words), and are disorganized in their thinking and other activities as they often lose track of the goal of their activities. They may be described as acting without hindsight or forethought, and are frequently less able to anticipate and prepare for future events.

Recent research suggests that those with ADHD cannot sense or use time as adequately in their daily activities as others. They often are late for appointments and deadlines, unprepared for upcoming activities, and less able to pursue long-term goals and plans. Problems with time management and organization for upcoming events are commonplace in older children and adults with the disorder (Barkley & Murphy, 2006). Children with ADHD also have poor planning and anticipation skills; have reduced sensitivity to errors; impaired verbal problem solving and self-directed speech; problems developing, using, and monitoring organizational strategies; and emotional self-regulation problems (Barkley, 2003).

The developmental progression also involves internalization of language. As the child matures, speech toward others is verbalized, often out loud, to one's self. It then progresses to subvocal self-speech and finally to fully covert or private speech that comprises verbal thought. Because it is verbal, many researchers in the science see EF as being social in nature.

Thomas E. Brown (n.d.) notes that the following executive functions are impaired in those with ADHD:

1. *Activation:* Organizing, prioritizing, and activating to work.

2. *Focus:* Focusing, sustaining, and shifting attention to tasks.

3. *Effort:* Regulating alertness, sustaining effort, and processing speed.

4. *Emotion:* Managing frustration and modulating emotions.

5. *Memory:* Utilizing working memory and accessing recall.

6. *Action:* Monitoring and self-regulating action.

Although there is not complete agreement of what is constituted by executive functions, most researchers agree that they include the brain circuits that prioritize, integrate, and regulate other cognitive functions (Brown, 2005). To describe the role of executive functions, Brown (2005) uses the analogy of an orchestra conductor whose job it is to organize and regulate the different sections of the orchestra to produce good music. Similarly, the executive functions serve to regulate and organize cognitive functioning. Gioia, Isquith, Guy, and Kenworthy (2000) define eight subdomains of executive function, a groundbreaking concept in their Behavior Rating Inventory of Executive Function (BRIEF). The Inhibit, Shift, and Emotional Control subdomains are grouped together to form an additional composite known as the Behavioral Regulation Index (BRI). Additionally, the subdomains Initiate, Working Memory, Plan/Organize, Organization of Materials, and Monitor provide a composite known as the Metacognition Index. These two composites are combined to obtain an overall Global Executive Composite (GEC). The Delis–Kaplan Executive Function System (D–KEFS; Delis, Kaplan, & Kramer, 2001) assesses key components of executive function within verbal and spatial modalities through subtests that involve the client/patient directly.

Coaching is an effective method for people to identify their strengths, needs, and goals. Setting long- and short-term goals, one can improve time-management, organizational, and other EF skills to meet life's objectives. Although a long-term goal can take several weeks, months, or even years, there can be an end in sight. Sometimes graphic charts and other visual organization systems can be very helpful. Instructional techniques that are relevant to EF can be found in Chapter 6 and Chapter 7.

Is ADHD Really Just One Thing?

Several researchers, especially Dr. Russell Barkley, have suggested that there is evidence to support the idea that inattention and impulsivity/restlessness may be two different disorders involving different brain centers.

Barkley (1997b) proposed a unifying theory with core symptoms of impulsivity or hyperactivity, putting aside inattention, because people with attention problems alone are thought to present a separate disorder not addressed by his theory. Therefore, the lack of inhibition or self-regulation is identified as the main deficit in Barkley's theory. This is referred to as *disinhibition*, which Barkley sees as the reason for four major child development problems: (a) working memory; (b) self-regulation of emotion, motivation, and arousal; (c) internalization of speech; and (d) the ability to reconstitute past events and anticipate future ones. Failure to develop these executive functions should lead to inadequate control over motor output and to the behaviors that define ADHD, according to his theory. He also addressed this concept in *ADHD and the Nature of Self-Control* (Barkley, 1997a).

This theory attempts to establish ADHD as a neurological-related disorder attributable to presumed impairments in specific brain areas. Scientists have known about these areas for years, such as the prefrontal (and interconnected striatal) systems. They have been frequently found in war and motor vehicle injuries, for example. The theory draws brain-behavior relationships between these sites of the brain and executive functioning problems displayed by affected individuals.

Greene, Loeber, and Lahey (1991) pointed out that the problems of restraint, such as impulsivity and motor restlessness can be observed by ages 2 or 3, but inattention is more evident when a child enters school. Attention is more related to persistence, prolongation, and the perception of time. It is a different set of problems. Inattention may be, according to this theory, a separate disorder. It is interesting to note that many primarily inattentive people are hypoactive or slow processors of information. They often have been referred to as "sluggish."

Barkley has been concerned for many years about the problems children with ADHD have with the subjective perception of time. Some studies have confirmed the idea that the reconstruction of time differs from affected children and controls (Barkley, Edwards,

Laneri, Fletcher, & Metevia, 2001; Barkley, Koplowitz, Anderson, & McMurray, 1997) and time understanding (Foley Nicpon, Wodrich, & Robinson Kurpius, 2004) using behavioral ratings of ADHD symptom severity. Research related to memory and time perception has produced findings consistent with Barkley's theory (Kerns & Price, 2001).

Prolongation of time is related to accessing memory and building a prediction of the future and being able to plan for it. This suggests that attention and executive function are closely related. Inattentive children often seem spacey and forgetful of time, are late, and forget appointments. They tend to daydream more. Inattentive people tend to drift from ongoing events and are rarely aggressive, disruptive, or impulsive. Of course, there are "combined types" that display all core symptoms.

One interesting finding of Barkley's regards the problems young children have keeping their hands off of things. They might play appropriately with the object, but they do so at the wrong time and/ or place. This is called *utilization behavior* and refers to the attraction that children find in objects to which they cannot resist responding. Utilization occurs when "the action performed with any object is object-appropriate, (but) . . . it is context inappropriate" (Goldberg & Podell, 1995, p. 92). For example, opening an umbrella in a confined indoor space represents utilization behavior. In a sense the child is bypassing accepted rules for behavior that he or she might know. Utilization behavior has been demonstrated in a series of case studies of patients with frontal lobe damage, which is the same area of the brain thought to be involved in ADHD.

Problems with restraint can be even greater when children have "deeper" brain problems. For example, some children are triggered by conflict or frustration beyond irritation to "explosiveness" (Greene, 2001). Greene's *The Explosive Child* is a book that explains how anger as a coexisting condition with ADHD can become very serious. This explosiveness often goes far beyond the routine oppositional behavior found in many people with problems restraining the expression of anger and disagreement.

Components of Attention

Attention may have important components. There are theoretical ways in which attention is broken down by neurologists and neuropsychologists. Zubin (1975) was the first researcher to point out that attention could be divided into different aspects or elements. Pribram and McGuinness (1975) described arousal, activation, and effort as main factors in attention. Arousal and focused, selective, and sustained attention are concepts that are frequently mentioned in the research literature. Sohlberg and Mateer (1989) sorted attention into the following categories:

1. *Focused attention* describes the ability to respond specifically to visual, auditory, or tactile input.

2. *Sustained attention* refers to the ability to maintain a response to input continuously. This may include vigilance, working memory, and mental control.

3. *Selective attention* is the ability to maintain a behavioral or cognitive "set" when faced with distraction. This requires *freedom from distractibility*, a much used and abused term in cognitive psychology.

4. *Alternating attention* is the ability to shift focus from one thing to another. This involves the ability to shift response requirements between different inputs.

5. *Divided attention* is the ability to respond at the same time to multiple task demands.

Is ADHD a Case of Inherited Impatient Temperament?

Because there is such a strong link between having ADHD and having a parent with ADHD in cases not involving neurological insult, one way of looking at the condition is similar to the way we look at breeds of other species. Just as science has proved that some breeds of the same animals may carry different traits, including temperament, humans may have a genetic predisposition to possess calmer or more excitable temperaments. Perhaps the brains of some persons, especially with the impulsive/motor restless type, are not really impaired, but reflect a range of developmental continuum. Perhaps genes are responsible for a smaller or less enriched and connected brain for restraint, so much so that the entire hormonal and nervous system is more excitable, fidgety, or lacking in restraint.

Many studies, including one by Graham, Rutter, and George (1973), have made a connection between babies with "difficult" temperaments and later adjustment difficulties. This is generally a compilation of parent ratings based on the early irritability, crying, fussiness, or sleep problems of infants. This concept has caused quite a controversy in the literature, where some researchers have been accused of creating a negative expectation that might be stigmatizing babies for later life. Kagan (1997), however, reported studies of fearfulness in infants, which appeared to be a stable, partially biological, objective characteristic of actual later behavior that correlated moderately with parent reports. Factors like calmness, irritability, fearfulness, and restlessness, might be noted in infancy with some continuation into later life.

Do People With ADHD Display Early Evolutionary Styles of Coping?

One writer (Hartmann, 1993) has suggested that people with ADHD are sharper and more vigilant because they are "hunters" who share alertness with our primordial ancestors. Thom Hartmann has proposed a hunter vs. farmer (gatherer) theory in relation to the origins of ADHD. The underlying idea is that what we call symptoms are really age-old adaptive behaviors. The hunter-farmer type theory is one of many representing the idea of "neuro-diversity," suggesting that people with psychiatrically identified symptoms are simply different and not deficient or damaged. This concept also has been used to explain conditions like Asperger's syndrome, a mild form of autism. It has been suggested that people with Asperger's syndrome simply have modern, highly evolved brains and poorer social skills. They are just different and not disabled (Baron-Cohen, 2000). For a review of Asperger's syndrome for parents and teachers see *School Success for Kids With Asperger's Syndrome* (Silverman & Weinfeld, 2007).

Clearly, people with ADHD and autism exhibit behaviors that affect living by making it more challenging for everyday functioning. These behaviors (such as not looking at people or playing with objects repetitively in isolation in autism, or making risky, impulsive decisions in ADHD) are not merely a difference but a challenging and often disabling condition. There are few real advantages to a disorder that limits daily survival, at least that research has demonstrated.

Hartmann (1993) suggests that humans were nomadic hunters for thousands of years, but that this changed as agriculture developed and more people became farmers. Supposedly, people with ADHD kept some of the older hunter characteristics. Neurodiversity as a concept applies here because hyperfocus of people with ADHD, according to this theory, is seen as strength. Hunters (mostly men) needed to be more vigilant than gatherers (mostly women). Hartmann thought that this gender difference is supported by the fact that ADHD is diagnosed in more than twice as often in boys as in girls.

Some research has been found to support this view. Eisenberg, Campbell, Gray, and Sorenson (2008) have demonstrated in some groups that vigilance provides a significant advantage to nomadic peoples based on genetic studies. The theory has been criticized because it fails to more specifically predict the wide range of behaviors found in ADHD or some of its maladaptive features. Hartmann's hunter vs. farmer theory was developed in an attempt to explain the behavior of his son, who has ADHD. In defending his theory he conceded that he never intended the fundamental concepts to be scientifically verifiable.

As parents, teachers, and other professionals working with kids who have ADHD, the more theoretical and practical information we know, the better able we are to understand and assist them at home, in school, and in other environments. More information on ADHD research can be found in Appendix B.

ADHD in the School Context

The problems associated with ADHD are widespread, but especially notable are school performance deficits. Many teachers indicate feeling unprepared to teach children with attention problems and desire more training and strategies to assist them in working more effectively with students with ADHD in the classroom. In a review of school-based interventions for children with ADHD, researchers indicated that while teacher interventions are effective in reducing ADHD-related behaviors, they are less effective in enhancing academic performance (Reid, Vasa, Maag, & Wright, 1994).

Underachievement and poor scholastic outcome are frequent among students with ADHD (DuPaul & Eckert, 1998). In comparison to the normal population, children with attention deficits are at relative risk with respect to academic and social failures in school settings (Barkley, 1990). Research also suggests that children with the primarily inattentive and combined type of ADHD demonstrate significant deficits in cognitive and achievement testing, lower grades, and increased use of special education resources compared with the general population (Todd et al., 2002).

It is estimated that more than half of the children with the primary diagnosis of ADHD have school-related struggles. Specifically, children with ADHD have significantly higher lifetime rates of school dysfunction and lower achievement than their peers. These difficulties include a higher likelihood of grade repetition, need for academic tutoring, or enrollment in a special class. Children with ADHD also are more likely to exhibit impairments in reading and academic achievement as well as higher rates of learning disabilities and school dysfunction (Biederman et al., 1996).

There also appears to be a long-term impact associated with these academic struggles during childhood. Childhood ADHD places individuals at a relative risk for an educational disadvantage throughout life. In adulthood, children diagnosed with ADHD complete less formal schooling than their peers. While nearly one quarter of children with attention deficits did not complete high school, only 2% of their peers did not complete high school. In addition, only 1% of children with ADHD completed a graduate degree, while 8% of their peers completed a graduate degree. (Manuzza, Klein, Bessler, Malloy, & Lapadula, 1993).

Children and adolescents with ADHD often struggle with their day-to-day activities. Inattention can have a profound affect on learning, personal relationships, productivity, personal safety, and self-esteem.

chapter 2

The History
of ADHD

A respected Indian mystic, His Holiness Sant Rajinder Singh Maharaj (2000), president of the International Human Unity Conferences, is quoted as follows:

> When Alexander the Great lay dying, he asked his physician to extend his life. With all the treasures he had amassed, the mighty conqueror could not trade them for the extension of his life by even one breath. When another conqueror, King Mahmud of India, lay on his deathbed, he had a revelation. He ordered that during his funeral procession he be carried through the streets with his arms outstretched and his palms upturned for all to see. When questioned by his ministers why he wanted to do this, the king replied, "I want all the people to see that when we die, no matter how much we amass in this life through conquest or other means, we ultimately must leave this world empty-handed."

While this perspective might seem morbid to some, it is important that we realize that we can find fulfillment in our lives, but where we put our attention is essential. We may not be able to count, control and monitor our breaths or heartbeats and mete them out, but we can guide our attention. Our attention is a treasure. Its direction and sustained focus is one of the few things we can control. (p. 2)

When we mention the term *ADHD* in everyday conversation, it often is followed by emotional controversy, as if we are discussing a relatively newly discovered, modern malady. ADHD is the most commonly diagnosed behavioral disorder of childhood. However, the key concepts described in the most current accepted definition of ADHD and its subtypes (DSM-IV-TR) have been debated for centuries.

In 493 BCE, Hippocrates, best described as a physician and general scientist, described persons who had "quickened responses to sensory experiences and rapid movement to next impression" ("Attention Deficit Disorder," n.d., ¶9). He attributed this condition to an overbalance of fire element in the body over water. The treatment at the time often took the form of dietary changes. He thought individuals should treat their systems using natural remedies: eating barley rather than wheat bread and fish rather than meat, consuming water drinks, and participating in many natural and diverse physical activities ("Attention Deficit Disorder," n.d.). More natural treatments for such maladies, especially dietary treatments, are coming back into popularity. As our natural world at the time of this writing is more polluted and aggravated by the greenhouse effect and global warming, more people are returning to an idealized concept of the natural soil as a safe haven of supply for the treatments of our ills. The emphasis on a natural and healing diet is again in resurgence. See Chapter 10 on alternative treatments for a balanced view of the research in these matters.

Attention issues also appeared in literature. In his writings, Shakespeare made reference to an adult with a "malady of attention," in *Henry VIII* ("Attention Deficit Disorder," n.d.). In 1845, Dr. Heinrich Hoffmann wrote a book of illustrated poems about children with negative behaviors for his 3-year-old. These stories were generally in the form of humorous moral lessons, but they were about conditions over which the children had little control, and, yet took the blame and responsibility. His book was called *Die Geschichte vom Zappel-Philipp* (*The Story of Fidgety Philip*; "Attention Deficit Disorder," n.d.). *Der Struwwelpeter*, another of his children's books, was a description of a little boy who could have had Attention Deficit Hyperactivity Disorder. This book became very popular in Europe and gained attention in the United States as well. A number of such books had socializing and moralizing intentions, but involved scary punishments for noncompliance to parental rules. An early description of ADHD (inattentive subtype), referred to as "mental restlessness," was described in a book of mental problems by Dr. Alexander Crichton in 1798 (Palmer & Finger, 2001). "Restlessness," as in "motor restlessness," is still used today to describe a major component of ADHD (Palmer & Finger 2001).

In the late 19th century, the English pediatrician, Sir George Frederic Still, considered to be England's first professor of childhood medicine, and Dr. Adolph Meyer studied individuals with traumatic brain injuries, and made a connection between the brain damage and the unruly behaviors exhibited by these patients. In a 1902 lecture series to the English Royal College of Physicians, Still described a group of children with significant behavioral problems. He thought these were hereditary and not caused by environmental or parenting causes. Dr. Still demonstrated that abnormal psychical conditions in children showed that "a morbid defect of moral control" was often associated with physical diseases.

From 1918 to 1919, the worldwide influenza pandemic left many survivors with encephalitis, which affected their neurological functions. By the 1920's scientists had linked the hyperactive behavior of children to having previously suffered viral encephalitis, which was common in England at that time. These functions included behavior problems that sound like ADHD in their descriptions. It is now known that some illnesses, especially those accompanied by high fevers that cause neurological damage, can result in symptoms we now describe as

ADHD. These after-effects of illnesses were called "Post-Encephalitic Behavior Disorders" in 1922.

Dr. Charles Bradley (1937) reported that a group of children with behavioral problems improved after being treated with the stimulant Benzedrine at the Bradley Home in Providence, RI, the first mental health/psychiatric hospital for children in the United States. Dr. Bradley was attempting to find a treatment for the headaches caused by a diagnostic procedure called a pneumoencephalogram by using the psychostimulant Benzedrine. Pneumoencephalography is a procedure in which cerebrospinal fluid is drained from around the brain and replaced with air, oxygen, or helium to allow the structure of the brain to show up more clearly on an X-ray picture. The procedure was introduced in 1919 by the American neurosurgeon Walter Dandy. Headaches and vomiting were common side effects. The Benzedrine did not do much for the headaches, but teachers noticed that some of the children taking it experienced a striking improvement in their schoolwork. The children themselves noticed the improvement and dubbed the medicine "arithmetic pills." Bradley and Bowen reported in 1940, in the *American Journal of Orthopsychiatry*, that 14 of 30 children with behavior problems showed a "spectacular change in behavior and remarkably improved school performance" during one week of treatment with Benzedrine (p. 582). His subsequent research and that of others established the benefit of psychostimulants in the treatment of ADHD.

Postencephalitic and other forms of brain damage led researchers and medical historians to believe that the condition we now know as ADHD was the result of injury rather than heredity. In 1960, Dr. Stella Chess described "Hyperactive Child Syndrome," attributing it to causes other than brain injury. This resulted in a controversy in the field. The idea of undetected brain lesions being responsible for neurological differences and disabilities persists today. The various neurological causes for ADHD and other disorders are being increasingly clarified through the rapidly evolving field of brain imaging technology.

Europeans saw hyperactivity as an atypicality associated with retardation, brain damage, and conduct disorders. Changes to the international medical diagnostic coding system (ICD), most often employed in Europe, were not made until 1994. The general label "Minimal Brain Damage" was employed in psychiatric diagnosis around 1960. U.S. researchers concluded around 1966 that the condition could not be traced to any observable or measurable brain disorder, so they changed the terminology from Minimal Brain Damage to Minimal Brain Dysfunction.

Psychiatry officially codified a condition called *hyperkinetic reaction of childhood* in 1968. The name Attention Deficit Disorder (ADD) was first introduced in the 1980 edition of DSM-III. By 1987 the DSM-IIIR was released, changing the diagnosis to "Undifferentiated Attention Deficit Disorder." Further revisions to the DSM were made in the 1994 DSM-IV describing three groupings within ADHD: mainly inattentive, mainly hyperactive-impulsive, and both in combination.

What we now refer to as ADHD combined type was the subject of increasing study in the 1960s and 1970s. The focus in the 1960s was primarily on hyperactivity. That emphasis changed in the 1970s when doctors and researchers began making the connection between apparent inward daydreaming and lack of focus and outward impulsivity and hyperactivity. By the 1990s, attention deficits became widely studied, discussed, debated, and diagnosed.

The stimulant methylphenidate was first produced in 1950 and commercially distributed as Ritalin in 1957. Methylphenidate is currently the primary ingredient in a number of medications under the names Focalin, Concerta, Metadate, and Methylin. Methylphenidate in its various forms still remains one of the most widely prescribed medications for ADHD. Initially, however, methylphenidate was used to treat narcolepsy, chronic fatigue, depression, and to counter the sedating effects of other medications.

However, there are controversial side effects and long-term implications of the use of medications. For example, in 1975, pemoline (Cylert) was approved by the FDA for use in the treatment of ADHD. It appeared to successfully address the symptoms, but it was traced to liver failure in research studies and was taken off the market 27 years after its introduction.

As ADHD was researched, it became clear that the United States appeared to be identifying a significantly higher number of cases than other countries. It was suggested that Americans, by nature of being a country of immigrants, are more restless. Research on the topic became increasingly intense. In 1996, ADHD accounted for approximately 40% of child psychiatry research references.

In 1999, one of the largest studies on children in history and the largest study of treatment for ADHD was published in the *American Journal of Psychiatry*. It is known as the National Institutes of Mental Health (NIMH) Multimodal Treatment Study of ADHD (MTA Study), and it studied more than 570 children with ADHD at six research sites in the United States and Canada, who were randomly assigned to four treatment groups. Results were surprising, showing that medication alone was more effective than psychological or social (psychosocial) treatments alone. However, the combination of pharmacological and psychosocial treatments was seen to be more helpful for some subgroups of children beyond the improvement achieved by medication alone. Numerous studies have been published based on the MTA dataset. The MTA study is described in greater detail in Appendix B.

Two important things have become clear from these studies:

1. Improvement in self-management at home, school, and community in the life of a child suffering from ADHD is best accomplished with the properly integrated use of selected treatments in a multimodal system, applied through the cooperation of stakeholders and caregivers across the child's life settings.

2. Improvements in school need to be carefully evaluated in terms of actual change in academic performance and social management as a result of these multimodal treatments, including the employment of prescriptive medications. The improvements, due to effects of medicine and other treatments, need to be care-

fully linked to real improvement in areas of life that matter for the child.

In the last decade a number of stimulants and other medications have been researched and prescribed. The use of medications has greatly accelerated during this time. In recent years, some concerns have emerged despite the finding of the MTA study, attributing the strongest positive effects to medication in an array of multiple treatment approaches. Atomoxetine (Strattera) received the first FDA approval for a nonstimulant drug to be used specifically for ADHD in 2003. In 2007, lisdexamfetamine (Vyvanse) became the first prodrug, or a drug given in a less active form, to receive FDA approval for ADHD.

This book is written at a time when the public, especially parents and professionals, are very confused about the effectiveness and safety of medications. Objective and exaggerated stories of side effects and the lethality of medications abound. Often parents are turning to unproven alternative treatments in the hope that a "return to nature" or a flight to newer technologies will solve their children's problems. High-tech approaches to management of the brain and behavior are being employed, such as biofeedback and cognitive training. Social skills groups are being formed. But, what is really effective?

We will see in later chapters that ADHD is becoming increasingly refined in its definition and in the discovery of brain/behavior connections. The authors of this book hope to clarify the issues, provide research support for solid ideas, dispel myths, and guide parents and educators toward effective, responsible approaches to an integrated care system that will show measurable changes in behavior and achievement.

chapter 3

The Medical Perspective*

"The only way to maximize potential for
performance is to be calm in the mind."
Brian Sipe, Former NFL MVP

PARENTS and professionals must
keep updated about the currently available medical options for individuals with ADHD in order to
make appropriate and educated decisions regarding treatment. The information within this chapter
is designed to provide medically relevant findings
and cutting-edge pharmaceutical interventions.
Additionally, questions that are frequently asked by
parents and professionals are answered and myths
are dispelled. The more we know and understand
about the medical view and treatment of ADHD,
the better able we are to determine the nature of
ADHD and what is effective in treating it.

---

* This chapter was contributed by Lance D. Clawson, M.D., F.A.A.C.A.P.

Facts Versus Fiction

Ever since Dr. Charles Bradley's research on the use of Benzedrine with children in the 1930's at the Emma Pendleton Bradley Hospital (see Chapter 2), ADHD has become one of the best-studied psychiatric disorders. What causes ADHD? How do we diagnose ADHD? What are the most effective treatments for ADHD? These are only some of the questions researchers have pursued. ADHD has gone by many names, as the last chapter pointed out, including hyperkinetic syndrome of childhood, hyperactive child syndrome, minimal brain dysfunction, Attention Deficit Disorder (ADD), and Attention Deficit Disorder with Hyperactivity (ADDH). The current label, Attention Deficit Hyperactivity Disorder (ADHD), came into being when the most recent version of the Diagnostic and Statistical Manual was published in 1994 (DSM-IV) by the American Psychiatric Association. As a result of the growing interest in this disorder, there are now more than 350 scientific studies describing the safety and effectiveness of a variety of medical treatments, particularly the class of medications known as psychostimulants (Connor & Meltzer, 2006; Pliszka & AACAP Work Group on Quality Issues, 2007).

Most exciting in the past decade has been the rapidly growing body of scientific evidence that shows that ADHD, for the vast majority of cases, is undeniably a heritable disorder of brain functioning. We have seen this in more recent studies using novel imaging technologies, where children with ADHD don't seem to be able to activate certain brain structures in response to specific tasks when compared to their non-ADHD peers, and how inheritance (genetics) plays such a large role in the etiology (cause) of the disorder.

Some have argued (albeit with little to support their opinion) that ADHD is not a "real" disorder, but actually something created by the medical community, and really is just a mislabeling of normal, spirited children. On the contrary, even prior to our ability to image the brains and examine the genes of individuals with ADHD, there were decades of well-designed, scientific studies showing that children with ADHD share certain features and can be reliably differentiated from their counterparts without ADHD. In fact, when reviewing the available information, ADHD is estimated to occur in approximately 7%–8% of the children in the United States (approximately 3 to 4 million children in total). When looking at ADHD in other countries, ADHD is reliably diagnosed in 3%–9% of the population. Thus, no matter what the culture, or differences in diagnostic approach, we see ADHD consistently around the planet (Barkley, 2006).

In 2005, the National Survey of Children's Health, conducted by the Centers of Disease Control and Prevention, asked 100,000 parents of youngsters ages 4 to 17 years if their children were ever diagnosed with or treated for ADHD. What they found was that out of all the children who would be presumed to have ADHD, *only 55% had ever been treated for the disorder* (U.S. Department of Health and Human Resources Services Administration, n.d.). This is a very important fact, because what has been debated often in the public arena has been the belief our children are overtreated, when in truth, we're only treating slightly more than half of those who truly need it.

The U. S. Surgeon General's report on the mental health of children (U.S. Public Health Service, 2001) identified that for all psychiatric disorders in children we are failing to provide adequate diagnosis and treatment for nearly 80% of them, and ADHD is the most common of these disorders.

Many also argue that ADHD is a benign condition that is outgrown by adolescence. In actuality, we now know, after observing these children for 20 years into adulthood, that, ADHD is anything but benign. The results of this "longitudinal" research are that children diagnosed with ADHD are at much greater risk for negative life outcomes in adolescence and adulthood. For many clinicians who treat this disorder, a common mantra is: "ADHD is a high-risk disorder and must be treated in order to protect these children."

As mentioned previously, children with ADHD, as they grow up, are much more likely to develop problems with substance abuse, experience motor vehicle accidents, develop sexually transmitted diseases and/or out-of-wedlock pregnancies, as well as suffer school failure and early school drop-out. In fact, it appears that even the health outcomes for adults with ADHD are identifiably worse as they age (Barkley, 2007). When medical costs associated with children with ADHD are analyzed, they are nearly twice that of children without ADHD (even when not adding in the costs of mental health treatment). These children are injured more frequently and more severely compared to children without ADHD (Leibson, Katusic, Barbaresi, Ransom, & O'Brien, 2001). Thus, ADHD is not a misnomer, describing spirited and creative children, but in truth, is a potentially dangerous disorder.

The underpinnings or etiology of ADHD are a set of neurological deficits. These deficits affect, to varying degrees, a child's ability to:

- imagine the outcomes of his or her behavioral choices (engage in mental time travel),

- inhibit impulses,

- maintain motivational states,

- develop a plan and implement this plan to achieve a desired goal,

- change strategies when unsuccessful,

- maintain focus on a particular task,

- organize thinking,

- regulate emotions,

- perceive the passage of time, and

- have the capacity to be self-observing and reflect on his or her current emotional and behavioral state.

A corollary to these deficit issues is that the brains of children with ADHD are in general underactive. Thus, many of these children seek high levels of stimulation to compensate for their underactive central nervous systems. This may then lead to engaging in high-risk or exciting behaviors regardless of consequences (because they have a deficit in predicting the future in relation to their behavior). This stimulus seeking may lead to reckless driving, impulsive use of drugs or alcohol, or seeming addiction to video/computer games, as a few examples. The brain regions that are seen as underactive and/or smaller are all intimately concerned with the problems with thinking, reflecting, and planning discussed above. As a result, an individual with ADHD requires a comprehensive approach of intervention to support their emotional and behavioral development.

Another frequent misconception of ADHD is that it can be "outgrown." Depending on how you measure ADHD symptoms, and whom you ask, the results vary. When interviewing both the adult with ADHD and his or her parents, using more modern criteria, it appears that 46%–66% individuals diagnosed with ADHD as children will still qualify for the full diagnosis as an adult. Now, if you only ask adults with ADHD regarding their symptoms and problems, without the benefit of outside observers who know them well, perhaps only 3%–12% identify themselves as suffering from the full disorder. Because we identified above that individuals with ADHD have difficulty with self-observation, it may come as no surprise that others see them as symptomatic, yet they may not fully perceive the impact of their behavior on others. Thus, perhaps nearly ⅔ of children diagnosed with ADHD will *not* outgrow the disorder, and will still qualify for the full syndrome. Of equal importance is that even when not qualifying for the full DSM disorder, adults diagnosed with ADHD in childhood will still describe functional impairment and significant life problems 85%–90% of the time due to ADHD symptoms (Barkley, 2007; Pliszka & AACAP Work Group on Quality Issues, 2007). Once again, ADHD appears to be a chronic and potentially serious condition.

Environmental and Medical Risks for ADHD

More recent scientific literature regarding the different causes of ADHD in children indicates that there are a number of factors that increase the likelihood that any given child will have ADHD. These include issues such as maternal smoking during pregnancy (increasing the odds of a child having ADHD by 2.5 times) and maternal alcohol drinking during pregnancy (again, increasing the odds by 2.5 that the child will have ADHD; Barkley, 2006). Barkley (2006) noted that other risk factors include the total number of complications during pregnancy (more complications increase the risk) and low birth weight and premature birth (very premature infants may experience bleeding in the brain; 45% of these children end up with ADHD).

Although the vast majority of ADHD is related to genetic causes and influenced by the risk factors noted above, approximately 3%–7% of ADHD cases are acquired due to illness or trauma (Barkley, 2006). A list of such acquired causes include head trauma, brain hypoxia (lack of oxygen or blood supply to the brain), brain tumors, and infection of the brain; lead poisoning in young children; brain damage caused by the treatments associated with acute lymphoblastic leukemia (ALL); postnatal streptococcal bacterial infection that triggers an autoimmune antibody attack of basal ganglia; and elevated levels of phenylalanine. (Phenylalanine is a naturally occurring amino acid found in breast milk, but is also added to a number of manufactured food products. Very high levels of phenylalanine in the blood of pregnant women are considered damaging to the brain of the developing child.)

Genetics of ADHD

If not due to a direct insult to the brain, ADHD is related to genetic factors. For instance, Barkley (2006) noted that if one child has ADHD, there is a 25%–35% chance that any of his or her siblings also will be affected. For identical twins, if one twin is diagnosed, the chance that the other twin also has ADHD is 78%–92% (Barkley, 2006). Another way to look at the heritability of ADHD is that if a child is diagnosed with ADHD, there is a 15%–20% chance that his or her mother also has ADHD and a 25%–30% chance that his or her father suffers from ADHD (Barkley, 2006). Finally, if one parent has

ADHD in a family, there is more than eight times the risk that any of his or her children also will have ADHD.

Scientists have utilized modern techniques to examine the human genome in order to determine what genes are responsible for the inheritance patterns for ADHD seen in families. As with many neuropsychiatric disorders it appears that ADHD is "multigenic," and that there are a number of possible genes that may be responsible alone or in combination for the transmission of ADHD. Although a full description of the genetic findings is beyond the scope of this chapter, many of the candidate genes studied are related to the production, metabolism, transport, and removal of the neurotransmitters known as dopamine and norepinephrine.

Current research has described a host of genes that may have a causal role in the development of ADHD. There are several forms of the DRD4 gene (a gene that codes for one of the dopamine receptors), which is related to novelty seeking and exploratory behavior. Certain long forms of the DRD4 gene blunt dopamine sensitivity. Three forms of the DAT1 gene (a gene that codes for one of the dopamine transporter proteins) have been implicated, but its function is not well understood. The DBH-TaqI gene produces an enzyme that helps convert dopamine to norepinephrine and the A2 form (called an allele) is connected to ADHD. One final major candidate gene is MAO-A, which produces a mitochondrial enzyme that regulates presynaptic dopamine signals and other neurotransmitter systems. In addition to these major candidates, there are 15 other minor genes that are considered possible candidates as well. We have recent evidence to support that there may also be "gene X environment" interactions as well. For instance, adolescents who have experienced significant psychosocial adversity have worse ADHD symptoms compared to those teens that have had fairly normal lives, even though both groups have the same allelic form of the DAT1 gene (Laucht et al., 2007). This is similar to what we have found in depressive disorders. If an individual has a certain "short" form (an allele) of a gene involved in the metabolism of serotonin, this individual will, in general, not develop depression unless they experience significant psychosocial adversity. Thus it appears that certain genes may place an individual at greater risk for ADHD (similar to the depression story) if they experience a hard life, but will fare much better if raised in a more normal environment. As we can see, there is still much to uncover about the specific role of each of these genes play and just what type of ADHD they transmit with regards to their course and treatment.

Brain Imaging

Imaging technology has lead to an acceleration of our knowledge regarding the differences in the ADHD brain. The primary techniques utilized in the study of ADHD are:

1. Magnetic Resonance Imaging (MRI), which gives a static picture of an individual's brain at a certain point in time.

2. Functional MRI (fMRI) gives an image of the brain at work, essentially showing the relative activity between the various brain structures by measuring the flow of blood to the different brain regions.

3. Positron Emission Tomography (PET) generates a picture of the brain based on the relative concentrations of a radio-labeled molecule across the brain. We can radio-label a variety of molecules to look at a brain from different vantage points. For example, radio-labeled glucose will be concentrated in those areas of the brain that are most actively using glucose during the time of the scan. SPECT (Single Positron Emission Tomography) is a simplified form of the PET scan, and reveals less detailed information on the current functional status of the brain.

4. Quantitative Electro-Encephalogram (QEEG) uses a computer to process the electrical signals emitted by the brain to give a picture of the relative activity of the various brain regions.

With imaging, what we see is that within the brain of the child with ADHD, a number of specific areas are smaller than children without ADHD, show less brain activity in these regions when comparing brains with and without ADHD, and appear less developed overall. The brain areas found to have these abnormalities are the Orbital-Prefrontal Cortex (seen primarily on the right side of the brain), the Basal Ganglia (seen mainly in two subareas of the Basal Ganglia, the striatum and the globus pallidus), and the Cerebellum (seen in the central vermis area of the cerebellum, more on the right side).

It also appears that the more abnormal these areas in question appear, the more severe the ADHD symptoms are, particularly with regards to patients' ability to inhibit responses on neuropsychological tests. There have been no differences in these findings when comparing boys and girls, and the findings persist with age, although recently, a percentage of young adults appear to improve when looking at the increase in the actual size of these areas over time (which is consistent with the previous discussion of how symptoms improve with age in a certain percentage of individuals). Finally, these findings are not related to having used stimulant medications (as these imaging results are the same between children with ADHD who have taken medication and those that have not; R. Barkley, personal communication, February 2008).

The current state of imaging technology cannot provide us with the information necessary to diagnose a single individual with ADHD. There are some physicians who claim that a single brain scan (e.g., SPECT or QEEG) can diagnose ADHD reliably along with a host of other disorders. These claims are not supported by research using more sensitive imaging techniques and more rigorous inquiries. The reality is that imaging findings so far are research-based and the results of these studies are based on the *combined statistically analyzed* findings in *groups* of patients with ADHD.

In other words, so far we have not found a way to take a single individual and use the available technology to "look" into his brain and definitely say what the picture means for that particular person. Yet, the search continues. One exciting example is the work by Jeffrey Newcorn, M.D., who is studying the patterns of activation in the brains of children with ADHD using fMRI to discover how we might be able to determine which individuals with ADHD might preferentially respond to the various ADHD medical treatments (J. Newcorn, personal communication, February 2008). Another promising example is the use of a radio-labeled compound, 123-Altropane. This molecule preferentially attaches to the dopamine transporter in the basal ganglia of the brain (both dopamine, a neurotransmitter, and the basal ganglia are considered central in the pathogenesis of ADHD). When injected into individuals with and without ADHD, higher concentrations of the 123-Altropane attached to the dopamine transporters in the basal ganglia appears to be a consistent finding in individuals with ADHD, suggesting that this may become a method whereby a single brain scan (SPECT) could help diagnose the presence of ADHD, but it is still experimental (Society of Nuclear Medicine, 2003). Exciting as these new technologies are, as clinicians, parents, and educators, it will be some time before their full potential will be realized.

Medication for ADHD

Medications are, the majority of the time, essential in improving the outcomes of children with ADHD. The best objective evidence for this assertion is the NIMH sponsored MTA study (see Appendix B for more information). This project is one of the most powerful research undertakings to date in studying ADHD. In the study, the children were divided into several groups: Those that received usual "community" treatment, those treated with stimulant medication 7 days a week for at least 12 hours per day, those given behavioral treatment but no medication, and finally a group receiving both behavioral treatments and medication. What we learned about children with ADHD through this study is that they don't significantly improve, regardless of what interventions are provided, until they are given consistent, daily, and adequate doses of medication (Jensen, 2005). These findings are not a surprise: Developmental pediatricians, child neurologists, and child and adolescent psychiatrists have supported this approach to medication "coverage" for more than a decade. Now, clinical wisdom and research findings have converged as children with ADHD receive both medical treatment and behavioral interventions.

Many parents and educators are concerned about giving children and teens medication for ADHD. Many of the concerns and misconceptions are brought up when the diagnosis is made and a clinician suggests medication. Frequent concerns are voiced and often include the following:

1. *My child won't learn to control himself, but will be dependent on the medication.* Although many parents express this concern, the MTA study, as well as a host of other research, suggests that learning and developing life skills occurs more readily when individuals with ADHD are taking medication and that such learning and positive changes do not readily occur without it.

2. *My child will develop drug problems later in life due to taking medication early on for ADHD.* Actually, the available literature on substance abuse indicates that the rates of substance abuse in ADHD is not affected by the prescription of stimulants beginning as early as age 6 or 7 years (Manuzza et al., 2008), and has been show in one instance to reduce the increased rate of substance use in individuals with ADHD.

3. *My child will have his personality changed with medications or he will be a "zombie."* Although an overmedicated child may appear sedated or "spacey," proper management of ADHD medications should not sedate or flatten a child's emotions excessively.

4. *Stimulant treatments will make my child shorter.* This is a frequent concern. First, when treating any child for ADHD, the physician must monitor the child and ensure that any appetite suppression by the medication is counterbalanced with adequate nutrition to ensure normal physical development. There has been conflicting evidence over the years regarding children with ADHD being shorter due to medication. It does appear now that predicted adult height may be affected by up to 1 inch, although this is still

a difficult conclusion to draw as children with ADHD may have comorbid conditions that also can affect predicted adult height.

5. *My child won't sleep well on the medication.* ADHD medications do, in a minority of children, cause difficulty in falling asleep, but the reality is that an estimated half of all children diagnosed with ADHD have chronic difficulty initiating sleep before any medication is provided, and that many times the problem with sleep may require some intervention. If sleep problems can be clearly linked to a particular medication regimen, then it makes sense to find another medication approach that is both effective and does not interfere with sleep initiation.

6. *The medication will damage my child's brain with chronic use.* Although this is an issue that has not been definitely answered with specific research, it is safe to say that we are fairly certain that after 80 years study, we know that the social, educational, and health outcomes are better for children who are medically treated for ADHD versus those who are medication free.

The caveat here is that any child treated for ADHD should be thoroughly evaluated and assessed not only for the presence of ADHD, but the comorbid conditions mentioned in Chapter 1, as they complicate the clinical picture and must be considered and treated as well if the child is going to truly benefit. Additionally, there are certain conditions that can masquerade as ADHD. These may make a child appear as though she is suffering from ADHD, but in fact she may have another condition that requires attention prior to ADHD being considered. There are a number of medical conditions that may affect a child's ability to pay attention. The vast majority of these scenarios are represented by the picture of a relatively normal child who, over weeks to months, is unable to attend in school and/or home. A situation where the symptoms are relatively acute should lead to a thorough medical evaluation to make sure that there is no underlying medical disease. We should remember that ADHD is chronic and unremitting. A careful medical and developmental history typically reveals that

ADHD symptoms have been present for years, not weeks or months. Of course, acquired ADHD can develop from a significant insult to the brain as discussed previously, and this would be an exception to this general rule.

There are two potentially chronic medical conditions that should be considered prior to finalizing a diagnosis of ADHD, and these are hyper- or hypothyroidism and chronic lead ingestion. Both are easily assessed with a simple blood test. Sleeping conditions also should be assessed for obstructive sleep apnea (OSA) and restless leg syndrome (RLS), medical conditions where an individual has chronically disrupted sleep due to periodic cessation of his breathing while asleep (OSA) or violent jerks of his limbs (RLS) while asleep. Although less common in children as compared to adults, questions regarding sleep and sleep quality are important in the evaluation of anyone with a diagnosis of ADHD.

Several other psychiatric conditions should always be investigated as well prior to finalizing any diagnosis of ADHD including covert substance abuse, depression, OCD, psychosis, and undisclosed physical or sexual abuse.

Thus, when considering medication, careful attention to the medical and developmental history of a child is essential. Although medicating children with ADHD often is seen as simple, each child diagnosed with ADHD is unique, with a unique constellation of ADHD symptoms and comorbidities. Medication always is only one part of a complete plan of treatment. Medication addresses the biological dimension, but a complete understanding of the child is essential as the psychological/emotional life and social functioning must be considered as well. Interventions such as individual, group, and family therapies and parent guidance should always be considered for each child diagnosed with ADHD. Along with the medical and psycho/social aspects of treatment, appropriate school interventions must be considered in detail. In many children with a diagnosis of ADHD, a variety of interventions will need to be put in place in addition to effective medication intervention. More information on ideal school environments is discussed in Chapter 6.

The Approval of Medications

The Food and Drug Administration (FDA) has regulatory authority over the development and marketing of new pharmaceuticals. Any medication that eventually makes it to your local pharmacy goes through an extensive process of evaluation and determination of its safety and effectiveness. Any novel medication is first tested in animals under a variety of doses and circumstances (Phase I trials). If the medication appears safe in animal models, it can then progress to human use, first administering it to normal volunteers to determine its tolerability and safety in humans across a variety of doses (Phase II trials). If these results are satisfactory, then the new drug is submitted for testing in humans who actually have the disease/condition that the drug is intended to treat. Once again, if the new medication appears safe and effective, it is then tested in large numbers in individuals with the condition in a "blinded, placebo controlled" fashion to once again establish its safety and that it does indeed treat the illness. Often, this phase (Phase III) of testing is accompanied by extended "open-label" trials designed to gather information about safety and tolerability of the drug over a 6–24 month time frame. Many thousands of molecules are screened and evaluated in the laboratory for every drug that makes it through the regulatory process. It takes years, and many hundreds of millions of dollars to bring a new medication to market.

Once the FDA has thoroughly evaluated the research trials for a new medication that has been submitted for human use, they either will accept or reject the drug company's claims as to safety and efficacy. If the FDA approves the application, the medication can then be marketed to the public and distributed through the nation's pharmacies. This is a very complex, detailed, and highly regulated process. The disease(s)/illness(es) that the drug is approved to treat are referred to as "on label indications" for use. Once a medication has been on the market and further research is conducted, often additional studies are submitted for review for approval of additional and novel indications. This has been demonstrated in psychiatry by the fact that many of the antidepressants on the market originally received FDA approval for treating major depressive disorder. Over time, additional studies have shown their usefulness in a wide variety of conditions such as obsessive-compulsive disorder, generalized anxiety disorder, social phobia, post-traumatic stress disorder, and others, depending on the medication in question.

Off-label use of a medication is when a physician uses an FDA approved medication for an illness that the FDA has not yet evaluated for that specific condition. For instance, although the new atypical antipsychotic medications have been used and shown to be helpful in the clinical realm (through small research trials and individual case studies) in treating adolescent onset bipolar disorder, the FDA had not approved any of these medications until recently when several of the manufacturers completed large-scale research trials showing their safety and effectiveness, and gained, or are in the process of gaining, approval for their medication in treating this illness in teenagers.

Parents often wonder why a particular treatment that has been accepted in clinical practice as effective for a particular illness remains off-label and does not received FDA approval. There are many reasons why the FDA approval process has lagged behind clinical use of these pharmaceuticals in children and adolescents in general. In my opinion, having participated in this process as a clinical researcher, there have been two major factors at work. The first has been a deep concern about conducting medical research using children from both the perspective of the approving bodies that monitor research, and parents who don't want their children to be considered "guinea pigs." This issue of ensuring our children's safety is a real concern, and one of the effects of this caution has been the slower pace of research of psychiatric medications in minors. The other major issue has been financial. Due to the tremendous cost of obtaining FDA approval for a medication and the complexities of working with child and adolescent research subjects, the pharmaceutical manufacturers have been reticent in past years to obtain additional FDA indications for kids. Fortunately, the Clinton administration offered inducements to pharmaceutical manufacturers in 1998 by passing the FDA's Pediatric Rule, whereby the FDA was able to require studies in children for new and already marketed medications, and the process began to get underway. This provision was renewed in 2002 through The Best Pharmaceuticals for Children Act, which has kept the research going at a reasonable pace (Connor & Meltzer, 2006). Although the past 10 years has resulted in more and more FDA indications for children, the late start, so-to-speak, has placed our specific research-based knowledge regarding psychiatric medications in children and teens at a disadvantage compared to the adult population. The good news in all of this is that because ADHD has been erroneously considered mainly a disease of children in the past, many of the medications used to treat ADHD were actually first evaluated in children, and it has only been relatively recent that adult indications have been obtained through FDA application.

Current Medications

Stimulants

Stimulants are a class of medication that, as mentioned previously, have been extensively tested and evaluated in the ADHD population. All of the stimulants that are mentioned here are FDA approved for the treatment of ADHD. Although there are many different stimulant medications available on the market, all available medications are based on one of two stimulant molecules. They are either amphetamine-based compounds or methylphenidate-based compounds. What determines the differences between the various medications is how they are absorbed and released into the body, thereby affecting how long it takes them to take effect and how long they last. Stimulants, are not, in general, medications that have to build up in your system; the effect that is received is for that particular dose for a certain period of time (the duration of the medication) on that particular day. Once a stimulant wears off, it is no longer providing benefit and the symptoms of ADHD are once again in full swing for the most part.

The response rate for stimulants is approximately 75% when used in children, although if both amphetamine and methylphenidate-based products are tried in a particular child, the response rate is about 90% (Barkley, 2006). When comparing methylphenidate-based products to amphetamine-based medications, it appears that certain groups of individuals prefer one to the other. Generally, 10%–20% will prefer using amphetamines, while another 10%–20% will prefer methylphenidate (Fisher, 2006). This usually is based on individual tolerance of the medication's side effects, as well a subjective sense of well-being, although objectively, symptom reduction may be very similar if given equivalent doses regardless of individual preference. It's important to note that a "response" is not necessarily a cure, but a significant improvement in many or at least some of the symptoms of ADHD. A child may respond to one type of stimulant preferentially from a symptom point of view as well as a side effect standpoint. Even with a response, ADHD symptoms may be completely controlled in an excellent responder, or simply improve or attenuate a number of the ADHD symptoms in a different child *while the medication is active*. It's important to keep in mind that once the stimulants wear off there is no further therapeutic effect.

The array of medications available can be confusing, and the differences among them may not be an issue in one child, yet may make quite a difference in another. Thus, your child's physician must get a sense of how sensitive your child is to the various medication types and delivery systems, as well as how strong of a responder to stimulants he or she is. Please refer to Table 1 to get an idea of the variety and core differences amongst the stimulants currently on the market in the U.S. Although the official duration of effect is listed below, for any individual child this may be shorter or longer by up to several hours depending on the rate of the absorption and metabolism of the medication in that particular individual.

What the extensive research on stimulants has shown overall is that the benefits reported include the following:

• increased concentration and persistence,

• decreased impulsivity and hyperactivity,

• increased work productivity,

Table 1
Medications Used With Children With ADHD

Methylphenidate-Based Products

Generic Name	Brand Name(s)	Duration	Dose/Release Technology
Methylphenidate HCL	Ritalin tabs, Methylin chewable, Methylin elixir	4 hours	Immediate release tablet, chewable tablet, or grape-flavored elixir
Methylphenidate HCL	Concerta	12 hours	Medication is released slowly via the OROS system for 6 hours and then slowly declines in the blood stream.
Methylphenidate HCL	Metadate CD or ER capsules	8 hours	CD is formulated in a "dual dose" preparation where 30% is released at time zero and 70% is released 4 hours later. ER is a preparation that is released slowly over 4 hours.
Methylphenidate HCL	Ritalin LA capsules	8 hours	Formulated in a "dual dose" preparation where 50% is released at time zero and 50% is released 4 hours later.
Methylphenidate HCL	Ritalin SR tablets	6–8 hours	Wax impregnated tablets, slowly released over 4 hours.
Dexmethylphenidate	Focalin tabs	4 hours	Immediate release tablet.
Dexmethylphenidate	Focalin XR capsules	8 hours	Formulated in a "dual dose" preparation where 50% is released at time zero and 50% is released 4 hours later.
Methylphenidate	Daytrana patch	12+ hours	Released slowly via a transdermal delivery patch

Table 1, continued

Amphetamine-Based Products

Generic Name	Brand Name(s)	Duration	Dose/Release Technology
Methamphetamine HCL	Desoxyn tablets	4 hours	Immediate release, infrequently used due to abuse liability.
Dextroamphetamine sulfate	Dexedrine tabs, Dextrostat tabs	4+ hours	Immediate release.
Dextroamphetamine sulfate	Dexedrine Spansule	8 hours	Approximately 50% is released at time of ingestion. The remainder is released over the next several hours.
Mixed amphetamine salts	Adderall tablets	4+ hours	Immediate release.
Mixed amphetamine salts: Extended release	Adderall XR capsules	12 hours	Formulated in "dual dose" preparation where 50% is released at time zero and 50% is released 4 hours later.
Lisdexamfetamine	Vyvanse capsules	12+ hours	Consists of a dexamphetamine molecule linked to a leucine molecule. Once in the gastrointestinal tract the bond is broken enzymatically and the dexamphetamine is slowly released into the bloodstream.

- better emotional control,

- decreased aggression and defiance,

- improved compliance and rule following,

- better working memory and internalized language (self-talk/self-reflection),

- improved handwriting and motor coordination,

- improved self-esteem, and

- improved peer acceptance and interactions.

These are largely what teachers, clinicians, and parents want to see in response to stimulant medications; yet, remember that these improvements vary across domains and are relative improvements, so that one child might improve tremendously in all areas, and another might have more modest improvements in several areas, showing a meaningful response, but not a "cure" for all of the symptoms. This is probably due to each child's individual biology, the severity of his or her ADHD symptoms, other comorbid conditions that may be complicating the picture, and the home/school environment.

Another important aspect of stimulant treatment is to keep the child on the medication as many hours of the day as is practical and during which the child does not incur significant side effects. This is done in order to maximize therapeutic effect. Even with a long-acting stimulant, many children require a late afternoon dose of short-acting stimulant (IR or immediate release) so we can treat the ADHD symptoms during the times of day when high-demand activities such as sports, homework, and family time occur. In the same light, dosing over the summer months can have significant therapeutic benefit and should be strongly considered given that ADHD is ever-present both in and outside of the classroom. Stimulants, or any medical treatment for ADHD should be continued as *long as required* into adulthood, because there is no magic cut-off when medical management is no longer necessary and your child can progress without medication.

Medication induced side effects are generally benign, and with regards to stimulants are related to the total dose. A very minimal amount of children (about 5%) cannot tolerate stimulant medication due to adverse side effects. The most common side effects often decrease over time. These include trouble sleeping, loss of appetite, headaches, and stomachaches. These may improve with time or with adjusting the amount and timing of the stimulant dose. The prescribing physician should be on the lookout for these as well as irritability, tearfulness, and nervous habits (which are seen more rarely). Even more rarely, motor tics will be induced with stimulants. Weight loss is another issue and should be monitored. There has been concern over the past decade about the potential for stimulants to have adverse effects on the heart in part due to their potential to increase heart rate and/or blood pressure in certain individuals. All individuals who are prescribed stimulant medication should be screened for cardiovascular abnormalities based on family and medical history and receive a thorough physical exam. As with any medication there are very rare events such as psychosis that require forewarning the family in case such an uncommon event were to occur.

Whenever a stimulant is prescribed, a full list of potential side effects is provided by the prescribing physician and/or dispensing pharmacy, and should be reviewed with the physician prior to their use. Although medication use in ADHD is a crucial aspect of managing ADHD, in a recent study it was shown that if parents and teachers consistently use behavioral management techniques the initiation of stimulant medications can be delayed (Boschert, 2008). The study also showed that when children were treated with stimulants, they were able to succeed on lower average weekly doses of medication compared to those who were not receiving the behavioral interventions (Boschert, 2008).

Nonstimulants

There is one FDA-approved nonstimulant medication on the market, named atomoxetine (Strattera). Instead of affecting the amounts of available dopamine in the brain in the way that stimulants work (specifically increasing the amount of dopamine, and to some extent norepinephrine, in the synaptic cleft between individual nerve cells), atomoxetine works solely by promoting an increase of norepinephrine in the synaptic cleft.

Since its FDA approval in 2003, Atomoxetine has been used in more than 3 million patients. It has been shown to be effective for kids, teens, and adults with ADHD. Several differences between stimulants and atomoxetine are important to note. Compared to stimulants, atomoxetine requires a "build up" period of several weeks prior to reaching its full clinical effect. Atomoxetine remains in the system and is active for nearly 24 hours, and approximately 65% of individuals treated with atomoxetine are determined to be responders vs. the somewhat higher rate of response with stimulant medications (Kemner, Starr, Ciccone, Hooper-Wood, & Crockett, 2005; Kratochvil, Heiligenstein, Dittmann, Spencer, & Biederman, 2002). Interestingly, there is a 75%+ positive response rate in individuals who have never received stimulants prior to taking atomoxetine, and a 55% response rate in cases previously treated with stimulants (Kemner et al., 2005; Kratochvil et al., 2002).

Although it takes a bit longer to take effect, and somewhat fewer individuals respond to atomoxetine, the benefits are quite similar to those observed with stimulants. There is some preliminary evidence that shows, when compared, certain individuals prefer either methylphenidate or atomoxetine medication about 20% of the time (Wilens, Hammerness, & Spencer, 2006). Atomoxetine has an improved side effect/outcome profile when compared to stimulants regarding sleep disturbance, potential to be abused, loss of appetite, worsened anxiety, worsening of motor tics, flattening of emotional expression, and morning and evening symptom control. Side effects that are relatively common when using atomoxetine include somnolence (a state of "near-sleep" or a strong desire to sleep), nausea, gastrointestinal distress, urinary hesitancy (in adults), constipation, and headaches. Rare instances of suicidal ideas have been reported, so atomoxetine carries the same cautions regarding this issue as all of the antidepressants, as well as caution in using this compound in individuals with comorbid bipolar disorder. As with any of the medications listed in this chapter, a full understanding of their potential risks and benefits should be reviewed with your prescribing physician.

Because both atomoxetine and stimulants address similar, but also potentially different aspects of the ADHD syndrome, it has become common in recent years to use both atomoxetine and stimulants together, as the outcome may be better in a subpopulation of individuals with ADHD compared to using either type of medication alone (Wilens et al., 2006). As mentioned before, it is advised that medications be used in combination with behavioral interventions.

A range of medications have been used in treating ADHD for decades in some instances, but have not been approved by the FDA as "indicated" for ADHD. These off-label medical treatments often have reasonably good research to support the effectiveness in helping to treat ADHD, but for a number of reasons, have not been submitted for FDA approval.

The first group of these medications is referred to as adrenergic agents. The two available in North America are clonidine (Catapres) and guanfacine (Tenex). Both of these medications were originally used to treat high blood pressure, but have been found, through controlled research studies, to be useful in treating the hyperactivity and impulsivity associated with ADHD. Although the risk of causing low blood pressure in children taking these medications is low, they should be monitored for these cardiovascular effects. Sedation, particularly with clonidine, is a common side effect, and there is some risk of rebound high blood pressure if the medication is stopped abruptly. Typically, both of these compounds have been used in combination with stimulant medications as they can reduce the hyperactivity and impulsivity of ADHD, avoiding the need to increase the stimulant dose, thus reducing the side effect burden of stimulants. Both are thought to increase the availability of norepinephrine in the brain. Guanfacine is also used to treat motor tics and clonidine has been used frequently at bedtime to assist with the sleep problems associated with ADHD and stimulant side effects. Neither medication is as robust in treating all of the various symptoms of ADHD when compared to stimulants, and both are currently being evaluated by the FDA for official approval in the treatment of ADHD.

Modafinil (Provigil) is a nonstimulant wakefulness/alertness promoting agent that is approved for the treatment of narcolepsy and several other sleep-related disorders. Although it has been used off-label since its release to treat certain instances of stimulant intolerant individuals with ADHD, more formal study has demonstrated a fairly robust response (although less than that seen with stimulants) in treating ADHD overall (Swanson et al., 2006). Although modafinil was initially felt to be "approvable" by the FDA in treating ADHD, concerns about the risk of a serious drug-related rash derailed its approval in 2007, and it remains an off-label intervention.

A variety of antidepressants have long been used as early as the 1970s as "second line" treatment for ADHD. The most widely used category in past years is called the Tricyclic Antidepressants (TCA). Prior to the release of the SSRI antidepressant medications (with the recognized brand names of Prozac, Zoloft, Paxil, Luvox, and Celexa), TCAs were the most widely used antidepressant type. This class of antidepressants causes an increase in both the serotonin and norepinephrine levels in the brain. Unfortunately, due to rare, but potentially serious cardiac effects, and the availability of new classes of antidepressants without these same cardiac concerns, the use of TCAs has fallen off dramatically during the past 20 years.

Among the TCAs, desipramine has the most research support for its use in ADHD, but it also was the specific TCA that generated the most concern regarding the cardiac effects in children. Other TCAs used with success in ADHD include imipramine, nortriptyline, and amytriptyline; although the response is typically not as robust as seen with stimulant medications, they can still be a useful adjunct to treatment in certain individuals when properly monitored.

Bupropion (Wellbutrin) is another antidepressant of a different basic chemical structure, but like many medications that increase norepinephrine in the brain (as well dopamine to a smaller degree), bupropion has shown itself to be effective in treating ADHD in several well-designed studies. Clinically, it does not generate the response level of stimulants, but can be very effective in stimulant-sensitive individuals if dosed properly.

Experimental Medications

The next category of medications are considered experimental in nature because there are early indications of success from "open-label" studies and small controlled research trials, but not the amount of data typically required for their common use in the clinical setting as of yet. One promising group of medications is cognitive enhancers. These are compounds used to treat dementia in the elderly including Alzheimer's, but have, in certain populations of individuals with ADHD, shown promise. The early data suggests that the magnitude of response is perhaps 25%–30% overall, but that the memory enhancing effects of these medications seems to improve the organization, reflection, and task follow-through in responders (Waxmonsky, 2002).

There also is quite a bit of interest in the past few years in the nicotine receptor (also called nicotinic receptor), related, in part to the observation of the linkage between ADHD and early tobacco use, and the observation that medications that affect the nicotinic receptor can have a advantageous effect on ADHD symptoms. One older compound, originally used for blood pressure control called Inversine (mecamylamine) was originally found to reduce the tics of Tourette syndrome (nicotine from tobacco also diminishes tic intensity) and has also been observed to improve mood and overall functioning in some individuals with ADHD. Again, early evidence points toward a significant rate of response in the treatment of ADHD, and it appears that the nicotinic agents, along with the other experimental medications mentioned above target some, but perhaps not all of the ADHD symptom complex, although much more study remains to be done.

Not all children with ADHD are identical, thus they will respond differentially to the various medications used to treat the disorder. Not uncommon in clinical practice (particularly in children who are complex with severe symptoms, or medication sensitive/intolerant to full therapeutic doses of stimulants) is the practice of combining two medications or even three in clinical practice in order to address the various symptoms. This has been commonplace in combining adrenergic agents with stimulants to help reduce impulsivity and emotional outbursts, without the need to continue to increase the stimulant dose. Bupropion has been commonly added into the mix, as has atomoxetine, when a stimulant and/or adrenergic agent are already on board. Unfortunately, there is little to no research data to support this common practice. Clinicians must rely on careful observation, monitoring, and experience to determine the relative benefit and weigh the costs of combination therapy, although when done properly, better outcomes have been attained on a case-by-case basis.

Treating Comorbid Conditions

One last issue to address in considering medications is the need to treat comorbid conditions. First, it is important to ensure that the medications used to treat ADHD do not worsen the co-occurring condition(s). For example, stimulants may worsen the symptoms in anxious children and may worsen symptoms in poorly controlled bipolar disorder. Similarly, atomoxetine or bupropion can theoretically worsen bipolar disorder.

The other consideration is to try to use ADHD medications that might actually help treat a comorbid condition(s). For instance, bupropion also can help in treating anxiety and depression, and atomoxetine has been shown to be more effective in anxious children with ADHD by alleviating anxiety symptoms.

The last consideration is to treat all conditions present and not confuse one problem for another. A depressed child often will have low motivation and poor concentration. Therefore, if we try to treat ADHD, no matter how good of a job we do, that child's motivation and concentration will not improve significantly until the depression is managed as well. If a child has both ADHD and obsessive-compulsive disorder, he may appear very inattentive, but this may be due to the OCD and not necessarily the ADHD. The reading teacher may describe a child with both ADHD and dyslexia as inattentive in class. This may be due to ADHD symptoms, but also may be secondary to the dyslexia itself and the fact that the child is overwhelmed in reading class due to the learning disability and not the ADHD.

Thus, careful diagnosis, thoughtful and comprehensive treatment, and regular monitoring are essential in order to succeed in treating the child with ADHD with significant comorbidities. Although all children on psychiatric medication should be monitored closely and regularly, in general, ADHD medications have limited adverse interactions with standard treatments for depression, anxiety, autism, Tourette syndrome, OCD, and bipolar disorder. One important exception is the interaction of TCAs and stimulants, which should be more closely monitored. Typically, for complex cases involving several medications and diagnoses, a physician specifically trained for this type of situation is required, such as a child and adolescent psychiatrist.

Future Research and Directions

There are many opportunities for medical research in the study of ADHD as there is much that we do not know about this disorder. An important focus is on the understanding the causes of ADHD on a genetic and neurochemical level. Developing a standardized methodology for the diagnosis of ADHD is essential to enhance our research outcomes, because it is difficult to compare research results if the patients chosen to participate haven't been diagnosed with ADHD in a standard fashion. One other promising area of research (which would assist in diagnosing ADHD in a standard fashion) is to determine biologic markers for ADHD with the aid of new genetic and imaging technologies. Other pressing areas of needed research regarding ADHD are the public health impact of this disease on society at large, the economy, the educational system, and the family, as well as the true incidence of the condition (Lesesne, Abramowitz, Perou, & Brann, 2000).

Why do parents and educators need to be aware of medical research into ADHD? We need to know more about the outcomes of children with ADHD and the outcomes they face as adults with and without treatment. Finally, we must determine effective and best practices for behavioral interventions, and what new medications can be found that more effectively treat ADHD.

chapter 4

What Parents Need to Know

"For only as we ourselves, as adults, actually move and have our being in the state of love, can we be appropriate models and guides for our children. What we are teaches the child far more than what we say, so we must be what we want our children to become."

Joseph Chilton Pearce,
Teaching Children to Love

PARENTING is hard work. It can be filled with times of great joy. But, there are, of course, times that challenge us as we work with our kids. In particular, parenting a child or adolescent with ADHD can be frustrating and exhausting. In order to effectively manage a child's condition, it is important to feel prepared by accessing information that will support the child and help him acquire the appropriate services to address the disorder.

At first parents often are confused and frustrated about clarifying their child's diagnosis and honestly being able to estimate the long-term challenges they and their child face. Gradually, these concerns are replaced by a desire to trust professionals they work with and to form alliances with the school and other key players (including relatives in some cases) to form a plan.

At this time the parents may be involved in damage control or healing the embarrassment they feel from their child's public demonstration of behavior and, all too often, early school rejection. The child also is facing growing self-esteem issues, such as peer rejection, especially in more severe cases. A child may not be invited to birthday parties or sleepovers with the other children in his class or neighborhood.

Clinical experience and research reflect parents' feelings of guilt when they understandably lose patience with their disabled child.

The Stress of Parenting a Child or Adolescent With ADHD

Parenting a child or adolescent with ADHD can be stressful. It often involves placing certain demands on the child such as requiring completion of homework and chores. However, children and adolescents with ADHD have difficulty complying with these requests and need to be frequently reminded and guided to complete such tasks.

Johnston and Mash (2001) reviewed research on families of children with ADHD and found that the presence of ADHD in children is associated with disturbances in family and marital functioning, disrupted parent-child relationships, negative parental cognitions about their children's behavior, reduced parenting self-efficacy, and increased levels of parenting stress and parental psychopathology. These associations are particularly common when the ADHD is co-occurring with conduct problems.

As a parent, it is important to avoid a negative cycle of interactions. This cycle may start when a parent gives a child multiple demands with which he or she does not comply due to lack of interest or inattention.

When the negative cycle exists, parents find themselves yelling at, punishing, and lecturing their children. Youngsters and teens with ADHD may respond with anger, noncompliance, or other disruptive behaviors. In such a cycle, even minor demands on the part of the parent or small infractions on the part of the child or teenager will trigger the negative interaction cycle. Furthermore, while teens often have developmentally appropriate desires for independence and freedom, teenagers with ADHD still require guidance and help with organization.

In order to interrupt the negative cycle that may be created by the inconsistency caused by variability in behavior, it is important for parents and their children to adopt a clear style of communication. Parents should explicitly state rules and expectations and establish a consistent system of rewards and consequences. Two-partner relationships should establish and maintain consistency in expectations and messages. Teenagers should be encouraged to verbally express their concerns in an acceptable manner rather than bottling up their feelings and allowing them to be expressed through negative behaviors. If family conflict continues, seeking professional help in the form of individual and/or family counseling or therapy from a qualified mental health professional can be immensely helpful. This is part of a multimodal wraparound plan to "cover all the bases," as emphasized in this book.

As a parent of a child with symptoms of ADHD, including difficulties paying attention, restlessness, and impulsivity, it can be difficult to know where to go for help. This chapter is intended to provide guidance on where to find assistance and how to effectively support a child with ADHD.

Where to Go for Help

Parents often find it helpful to speak first with their child's pediatrician or family doctor about their concerns. Although some pediatricians may complete an assessment themselves, they often refer families to a mental health specialist whom they know and trust.

During the evaluation, parents should share any relevant information that may help the clinician accurately understand the child's developmental history. It is helpful to compose a typed developmental history of the child with relevant information so that the important facts are remembered. Share details surrounding pregnancy, the birth, developmental milestones, and the child's medical issues and procedures. Describe in detail the concerns about his or her symptoms in various settings including the home, school, and social environment. Additionally, parents should bring assessments or reports that are relevant including medical or school evaluations (see Appendix B for information about the diagnostic assessment process for children with symptoms that appear to be like ADHD). Keeping a school and medical folder on your child can be very helpful to professionals later.

If the child is diagnosed with ADHD after the evaluation, it is frequently beneficial to share the information that is gained through the evaluation with the child's teachers. Such information may include the child's cognitive and academic profile, his or her diagnosis, and recommendations made by the clinician, particularly those related to the school environment. Whether the child is in preschool or in college, or any grade in between, this information can be very helpful for teachers to assist the child in achieving success. In addition to talking to the child's teachers, parents should speak with a guidance counselor at the school to determine what can be done to support the child. For example, some children with ADHD are provided tutoring, counseling, or a mentor in the school setting. Often this sharing and assignment of supports will take place at a formal meeting at the school.

Daily Management of the Child with ADHD

Parents need to know that unconditional love is the most important thing and must be preserved. This is done through planned ignoring of negative behaviors, forgiveness, and reinforcing of positive behaviors. This means that both partners, when there are two, must agree to this philosophy and must work together through consistency and teamwork.

Parents need to learn principles of behavior modification. They need to use safe rewards that are powerful enough to retain their value. They need to know reward preferences and intervals. Some kids need rewards every few minutes and some every week. Punishment should be avoided unless absolutely necessary. Safe punishments such as time out can be employed. Rewards and positive experiences in general should far outweigh punishments.

When there are glitches, the day should be analyzed in 15 minute intervals or in naturally occurring event sequences, such as getting up, washing up, showering or bathing, brushing teeth, getting to the breakfast table in time, and getting to school on time. Behavior management plans require flexibility in monitoring and making needed adjustments for each child.

Daily Living for the Child With ADHD

Children with ADHD benefit from having a structured schedule with the same routine each weekday from morning until bedtime. The schedule should be posted in a location that everyone in the family can see. Activities should include school, homework, playtime, chores, afterschool activities, and family meals. When changes are made to the schedule, the child should be informed as far in advance as possible and the change must be posted on the schedule. Household chores also should be listed and posted with a place for chores to be marked off after the child completes them.

Praise and encouragement, as well as a consistent system of expectations and consequences, are very important. Children with ADHD require consistent rules that they understand and can follow. When children follow the rules, small rewards can be given. Such rewards do not have to be material in nature, but can include an extra book at nighttime, a choice of where to eat dinner, or having a sleepover with a friend. Rewards can reflect creative thinking; consult the child or teenager for their ideas. Because children with ADHD frequently receive criticism from others, they are accustomed to and expect negative feedback. It is important to look for good behavior and to praise the child. Praise that is specific and immediate will go a long way toward increasing the frequency of the desired behavior.

Organizing the Life of the Child with ADHD

Daily reminder checklists and reward charts can be placed on the inside door of your child's room or a conspicuous place such as the refrigerator door. The latter can be problematic, especially if the child's siblings do not receive similar rewards.

Rewards also should be based on the home/school contract (see Appendix A) in the multimodal plan as provided by the teacher in concert with you, the parent(s). This contract is more effective, of course, if the child has been involved in its development and "buys into" the target behavior objectives and rewards. The homeschool contract is discussed in Chapters 5 and 6 and Appendix A.

Dealing With Your Child's Anxiety

Because ADHD often coexists with anxiety, there are several forms of anxiety that parents may observe in their children. One form of anxiety is generalized anxiety. This is more chronic and more "hardwired" as a coexisting condition. It is one form of anxiety that may respond best to medication as prescribed by a knowledgeable physician. Sometimes a physician will choose one or more medications that can address the ADHD and anxiety at the same time.

Social anxiety often is present because the child may have more immature interpersonal skills or may lack coping skills exacerbated by peer rejection. Social anxiety might be seen more frequently in primarily inattentive children, especially those who are shy. And, social anxiety simply may be a part of a picture that is characterized by a general lack or weakness in social skills.

Anxiety also arises when there is the experience or anticipation of being overwhelmed by too much information, novelty, or complexity. This can happen in preparing for tests, especially because children with ADHD often need to read test instructions over and over to "register" the gist of the instruction or to comprehend the key ideas. Specific anxiety reduction or relaxation strategies may be beneficial.

One of the most challenging experiences and displays of anxiety is spiraling anxiety, where the child feels out of control because of worry, panic, or generally being overwhelmed by internal and/or external demands. A calm place or calming technique may need to be employed. Some arousal control systems are found in occupational therapy; for example, for younger children with very severe attention issues weighted vests or the use of direct contact as physical stimulation to the child will be used to control arousal. Some practitioners believe that Brain Gym®, yoga, or other such activities can activate greater calmness or smoothness in self-control. Sometimes a simple meditation technique also might be helpful in stabilizing and recentering your child. These solutions are described and explained further in Chapter 10.

Dealing With Oppositional Behavior

We know that oppositional behavior is found in a high percentage of children with ADHD, especially combined type. The multimodal plan in Chapter 5 addresses some parent training programs for dealing with these behaviors. In some cases, kids with ADHD may have more than oppositional behaviors. ADHD may coexist with a more pervasive form of behavior called *oppositional defiant disorder*, generally referred to as ODD. People with ODD learn, unfortunately, through trial and error of making interpersonal mistakes and creating conflict. They usually are argumentative and provoke frequent confrontations. They don't seem to learn well by preventive warnings, but by repeated social mistakes. This often is accompanied by rigidity and stubbornness and, when taking direction from parents and teachers, resistance and refusal.

Opposition generally can be dealt with to some extent through planned ignoring, having accurate expectations of how stressors will be addressed, and through planning to avoid trying situations before they arise. Opposition generally is accompanied by rigidity and stubbornness. These are not necessarily active choices that the child is making. Many children "lock up" and become oppositional or defiant when faced with stress. Locking up is a way of handling the feeling of being overwhelmed, which stems from the complexity of information or demands for responses the child is experiencing.

It is best to provide time for release of the emotion and the frustration that leads to oppositional behavior and the provision of positive consequences for more effective behaviors. These can be anticipated when the child has a co-occurring learning disability, for example. Academic resistance and "shutting down" can be seen whenever anyone is unable to approach, understand, or master a task set before him or her.

With children who have oppositional behaviors or the characteristics of ODD, power struggles are to be avoided. When possible offer clear, positive alternative behavior choices, which can be more rewarding or reinforced.

Handling Social Skills Deficits

Because social skill deficits are at the core of social immaturity found in ADHD, parents might experience frustration in helping their child initiate and maintain friendships and avoid peer rejection.

Scouts, team sports, social clubs, and interest groups that match a child's areas of expertise and passion can be helpful. Some afterschool groups are geared to include children who need some extra support. As far as sports are concerned, individual sports may be more appropriate in some cases, so that a child can compete with her own record.

Social skill therapy groups frequently are geared specifically for children with ADHD as described in the multimodal plan in Chapter 5. Much repetition of directly taught, specific skills may be required. This may involve rehearsal and modeling of successful social exchanges. Children with ADHD can be encouraged to use a required social chain of events, such as in table games that require taking turns.

Teaching Manners

Many children with ADHD fail to practice good private hygiene behavior or manners due to forgetfulness, lack of organization, or impulsivity.

A Web site called *Teacher Planet* has a wide range of resources on etiquette for children (visit http://www.teacherplanet.com/resource/manners.php). Some of these resources include visual posters that can be mounted on a wall and used to reinforce good manners. In some areas, consultants are available to teach manners through direct instruction. For example, a class could be taught to model a formal dinner party using proper etiquette, a scenario that would introduce multiple social skills opportunities.

At home, you also can outline and review general rules for good hygiene behavior and manners. You should teach your child what is private hygiene behavior (such as always using toilet paper when visiting the restroom) and what is public hygiene behavior (such as covering one's mouth when coughing). It also is easy for a child with ADHD to forget to say "please" and "thank you" when appropriate. Thus, there need to be reminders to help children practice these good manners. As in all instruction for kids, especially those with ADHD, correction needs to be gentle but firm and immediate. Reminding a child of what he or she did yesterday will not be as effective. Checklists and rewards and consequence programs also can be implemented to teach these skills.

Probably the biggest social problem with children with ADHD is impulsivity in judgment. We all need to learn to think first, count to five, or find some other manner for considering behaviors, especially communications, prior to their expression. Reminding children to "stop and think" is a good mantra for ensuring positive communication and other actions.

Managing Attention at Home

Managing attention at home should be directly coordinated with the same techniques as managing it at school (see Chapter 6). Using a multimodal plan, the same language and techniques should be employed consistently throughout the child's day at home and at school.

Generally, the parent should be prepared to recue frequently and to avoid very lengthy instructions, instead using directions in shorter steps or fewer units sequentially. One-on-one support should be done through proximity, such as in the kitchen or workshop, where the child can receive direct instruction, modeling, monitoring, feedback, and reward.

Preschool Thoughts

Parents get concerned when their toddler or preschool child is seemingly overactive or flits from one activity to another. As noted in Chapter 5, it is difficult, even for professionals, to determine when activity level and shifts in attention are developmentally excessive. Boys especially are a concern when they appear to be "too physical" or change interests rapidly when exploring their environment. It is a fact, however, that all preschool children change interests rapidly when exploring their environment and objects or activities in it. One significant marker of continuing problems is preschool expulsion, which is found in the records of many children whose problems persist.

Understanding Parental Concerns

After preschool is when parental concerns crystallize. This is especially true when oppositional behavior persists beyond age 4 (experienced child clinicians will testify that the "terrible twos" can persist through age 4). Because a high percentage of children with ADHD display oppositional behavior, when these behaviors persist further school and social challenges may be in store. It also is more clear how challenging children with ADHD can be when observing and interviewing parents. Parents, especially mothers, are worried, frustrated, and often distraught. They feel helpless in the face of their child's out-of-control behavior. They are embarrassed by their child's social rejection and teacher comments. In fact, some parent rating scales, such as the Parenting Stress Index (3rd ed.), created by Richard R. Abidin, are used to assess levels of such frustration. Many parents eventually will benefit from counseling or consultation on how to manage their challenging child.

For a very thorough, comprehensive, research-based volume on support to parents, take a look at *Taking Charge of ADHD: The Complete Authoritative Guide for Parents* by Russell Barkley (2000b). Dr. Barkley also has developed parent-training programs for parents of defiant children.

When concerns become persistent, parents seek help. In some jurisdictions, there are "child find" clinics that provide free or reduced cost developmental screenings including those for ADHD related behaviors. Such behaviors often are embedded in complicated behavioral and parent management problems. Because babies do not come with a manual, many young parents simply do not know what to expect from their child. All parents have to make decisions about how to handle their children using their best judgment. So, it is with confusion and trepidation that many parents present their young child to their doctor with these concerns, especially when there are so many possible causes for these behaviors. For example, some children whose language skills are delayed may get their peers' attention by hitting them because of frustration with their inability to communicate.

Using scientific knowledge, a finding can be classified in several ways, including true negatives, true positives, false negatives, and false positives. For example, a true negative is when the doctor realizes that a child does not have ADHD. A true positive is when the doctor concludes that a child who appears to have ADHD does in fact have it. In early meetings with the pediatrician it is hoped that true positives and true negatives are identified. Overmedication occurs often with false positives and lack of intervention can occur with a false negative.

Although pediatricians and child psychiatrists make increasingly more informed and correct diagnoses, misdiagnosis at the entry level into the system can and does occur. Schools may play it safe by labeling children "developmentally delayed" when the label of "Other Health Impaired," used to classify children with ADHD for special education services, is not yet deemed appropriate.

One of the most frequent concerns of parents is "Does my child need Ritalin?" The question displays the parent's need for information regarding the wide range of interventions and pharmacological options. The frequency of this question is one of the major reasons that this book was written. Parents need clear information on ADHD. They need to know that they can be part of an effective multimodal plan, and that there is a range of pharmacological options as part of such a plan. They need to understand that medication is not the only answer and that medication must be intelligently prescribed and managed. Chapter 3 provides detailed information on medical treatments of ADHD, and parents also should discuss such medical treatment with their child's pediatrician or family physician.

Requesting a School Evaluation

If the child has been having school problems, parents have the option to talk to school personnel about having the child evaluated at the school. Parents also may ask the staff, including the guidance counselor or school psychologist, for a referral to a qualified professional for testing outside of the school setting.

Some states require schools to evaluate children with symptoms of ADHD to determine if the symptoms are affecting the student's schoolwork and his or her social interactions with other students and teachers. The teacher can assist the parent in contacting the correct person at the school to request an evaluation. A formal request must be made in writing and include the parent's name, child's name, date the letter was written, and the reason for requesting the evaluation. The parent should make and keep a copy of the letter as a record.

In past years, school systems were hesitant to evaluate a child for ADHD. However, recent laws require schools to do an evaluation if ADHD is adversely impacting the student's performance in school. Decisions related to medication are not made through the school evaluation process. These decisions are for each family to make in consultation with their physician. When working with family doctors and any other professionals, parents need to discuss any services that the school is providing. This conversation will help the parent and doctor determine the best treatment plan for the child.

Accommodations and Other Supports

Individuals within the educational community, including policy makers and educators, have become increasingly aware of the significant learning problems associated with ADHD (WrightsLaw, n.d.). Due to these implications in the educational setting, various documents have been drafted by the federal government that specify the responsibilities of the local and state governments in addressing the academic needs of children with ADHD. Throughout the 1990s, the government established national educational goals and a program entitled *AMERICA 2000* to ensure that students with ADHD would receive educational services that would make them more likely to achieve their full potential. These goals were established with the understanding that every child is to be encouraged to learn and benefit from education. The goals emphasize that the educational community is responsible for working to improve learning opportunities for all children. Based upon this same rationale, children with ADHD typically are eligible for accommodations or services under one of two federal laws: the Individuals with Disabilities Education Act (IDEA) or Section 504 of the Rehabilitation Act of 1973, both of which are described briefly below.

Individuals With Disabilities Education Act

Some individuals with ADHD are eligible for special education services under Part B of IDEA. IDEA and subsequent federal regulations established several categories for special education eligibility with accompanying criteria for each. Of these categories for eligibility, students with ADHD typically meet the criteria for the eligibility code of "other health impaired," which requires "having limited strength, vitality or alertness, including a heightened alertness to environmental stimuli, that results in limited alertness with respect to the educational environment," in this case, due to ADHD that "adversely affects a child's educational performance" (IDEA, 2006, 34 C.F.R. 300.7 [a] [1]). IDEA acknowledges free and appropriate public education and related services designated in each child's Individualized Education Program (IEP).

If a student with ADHD qualifies for special education services, the school is required by law to design and implement an IEP. In developing the IEP, the school will evaluate the student's strengths and weaknesses and work with the parent to develop a comprehensive program individualized to the student's needs. A parent has the right to review the child's IEP periodically and approve the program or discuss concerns and recommendations.

The Rehabilitation Act–Section 504 Plan

Section 504 of the Rehabilitation Act of 1973 is a civil rights statute that protects students from being discriminated against because of their disability and requires that local education agencies develop individual 504 Plans for each child that meets the criteria of this act. In order for a child to be eligible for Section 504, an identified physical or mental condition that substantially limits a major life activity must exist. Many children with ADHD are not found eligible for services under IDEA because it requires a student to have both a disability and a need for special education and related services. However, some of these students who have the disability, but do not need services under IDEA, may be eligible for protection under Section 504. Section 504 is more general than IDEA because its protection extends beyond the category created by IDEA in terms of the students who qualify. The definition of disability is broader under Section 504 than IDEA. Although Section 504 also covers all students who qualify for services under IDEA, not all students who qualify for Section 504 meet the criteria for IDEA. Section 504, unlike IDEA, does not require the school to provide an IEP designed to meet the unique individual needs of the child. The Supreme Court has interpreted IDEA to require that appropriate education must confer educational benefit. Additionally, IDEA, unlike Section 504, provides a number of due process and procedural safeguards for parents who do not agree that their child is receiving educational benefits.

Provisions of IDEA and Section 504

IDEA and Section 504 are legal guidelines that are intended to ensure that children with ADHD receive an appropriate education. These regulations hold schools responsible for assuring that children with ADHD receive special education and related services. Although special educators teach some children with ADHD, a substantial number of general educators also are responsible for implementing the guidelines required by IEPs and Section 504 plans. Approximately 80% of children with ADHD are predominantly educated in a general

education classroom and only 50% receive any special education services (Reid et al., 1994). Therefore, Reid and Maag (1998) concluded
that general educators are becoming increasingly responsible for implementing and modifying accommodations for children with ADHD.

Encouraging Achievement

Often, students' poor school performance may not be related to
their disability alone—they also may be displaying underachievement.
Frequently, parents may be so careful to ensure protection for their
children with disabilities that they fail to set high standards for them.
We are not suggesting that children should be pushed beyond their
limits. Many persons unfamiliar with the complexities of special education issues may oversimplify problems with achievement by suggesting that "if she worked harder, she would be fine." Underachievement
can be a problem at all ability levels, whether students are disabled or
not. It is important to remember that adults are responsible to some
extent for their own happiness, but children require emotional protection and have a right to experience happiness. They also require
moral, character, and spiritual guidance to make positive life choices.
Commonly assumed markers of achievement should not violate their
rights for emotional protection, the experience of happiness, or the
ability to think for themselves about their life purposes.

Home-Related Achievement Issues

Parental attitude in the home is the key to encouraging school
achievement. We hope we love our children unconditionally, but every
child can be frustrating at times. For that reason, parents need to con-
tinually evaluate their feelings toward their child.

At times, parents may harbor feelings of resentment or even rejection toward their child with ADHD, which in turn are responsible for
guilty feelings and irrational responses.

Are there barriers to demonstrating unconditional love? Parents can be conveying unconditional love to their child even when they are disagreeing or correcting their child's behavior. Remember, a child's behavior might be bad, but the child isn't. For too many children, shame results from feeling as though they are fundamentally bad. Shame, even for short periods, is one of the most destructive emotions a child can feel. Making a child with disabilities feel shame for something out of his control is abusive. There are parents whose ability to love their child is temporarily blocked due to their own concerns, anxieties, and frustrations. This is, in some way, to be expected when one is rearing a child with ADHD. Honesty with one's self is very important. There is no perfect way to feel about the situation. Just remember that love emerges when the truth is confronted honestly.

Here are some further pointers for encouraging achievement:

- Every child can be seen as a unique gift with unique potential.

- Avoid comparing the child to other children. Let the child know that he has a duty to know his own strengths and make his best efforts in and out of the classroom.

- Not every child can be the best at everything, but he can be his best at something. Many very competent children have low expectations for themselves because the bar has been set too low. This is especially the case in children with disabilities—too many parents are happy to see their children just getting by. If a child is currently an underachiever, convey the firm belief and expectation that she can learn and excel.

- In being a reasonable advocate, be sure that accommodations, supports, and special instructional strategies are in place to make learning easier, but do not relieve the child from her responsibility to make reasonable efforts.

- Know the child's strengths and weaknesses. Eventually, a child's strengths will emerge, coalesce, and integrate into a unique mix that many parents enjoy and treasure and will lead to the child's feeling of competence and accomplishment.

- Decrease marital and family conflict that can cause roadblocks and resistance to emotional growth and growth and motivation to learn.

- Adult partners should talk about their views and expectations of their children and their family priorities.

- Parents should never argue about their child in front of him or her.

- Parents should seek to maximize points of agreement and learn to agree where they disagree. Put the "small stuff" aside. Make discussions a safe place to forge a shared philosophy about child rearing. Try to be on the same page as much as possible about child rearing practices, rules, and consequences. When there are great disparities between parental expectations, children lock up or learn to fail as a way to passively punish parents for not communicating effectively.

- Provide a sense of harmony in the home that fosters a desire to be there. Try to eat one meal together daily as a family and plan at-home family events such as regular game or movie nights.

- Success feels good. Children are born loving to learn and master challenges. Reward a child's successes with praise in a meaningful and genuine way so that she learns to know the feeling derived from mastering her challenges.

- Activities with intrinsic incentives often are higher and more enduring rewards than prizes.

- Be patient with the child. A positive self-concept as a learner takes time for a child who has been experiencing little success. It may take a while before the positive experience of academic success takes hold.

- Limit television and video game time to one hour per weekday and 1½ hours per weekend day. Parents also should limit telephone, instant messaging, and computer time.

- Make sure the child gets adequate sleep by turning in nightly at a reasonable hour. Try not to break this rule on the weekends.

- Be open to mental health consultation for significant problems and to receiving parenting counseling. Attend support groups where available or help create one in the area.

- Make sure the child knows the rules for home behavior and responsibilities. Have them written out and posted in the child's room until she has mastered them.

- Develop a "To Do" list to post inside the child's bedroom door with a check-off system. Parents may want to update this weekly as the child receives assignments from school, or even daily.

- Remember that children see structure and limits as part of being loved. They are uncomfortable, confused, and even frightened without clear limits and expectations.

- Be a benevolent dictator first, and a friend later, when rules are established. Freedom should be earned through demonstrated responsibility.

- Parents should model the behavior and values expected from the child in their own day-to-day activities, behavior, and conversation.

- Regularly demonstrate affection, especially with teenagers. Parents should tell their children often that they love them.

- Evaluate the openness of communication with the child through regular conversations. Children need to feel a parent's benign presence and acceptance through regular communication.

- Parents should be in regular contact with their child's school. Try to keep one teacher, special educator, administrator, or counselor as a pivotal information conduit. Use voicemail, e-mail, or any form of communication that is convenient for the school representative, and always communicate on an agreed-upon schedule for setting up meetings about the child. Establish good communication boundaries with your school representative and stick to them. This is part of the multimodal plan explained in Chapter 5.

- Parents should set up homework rules and guidelines.

- Come to an agreement with the child on regular study times every day for homework.

- Break up homework periods with dinner, snack, or exercise breaks.

- Encourage the child to communicate about homework problems or questions with friends through telephone, instant messaging, or study groups.

- A parent's attitude toward school can make all the difference in a child's achievement. Convey to the child that school is an honorable place, that teachers are worthy of respect, and that learning is their major job, second only to being a good human being.

- Volunteer to help out at school at least once a month, even with (or especially with) menial tasks. Let the school staff provide you with the work they need done. Volunteering should be controlled by the school and not by the parents' ideas of what the school needs. Volunteering shows children that their parents value school as a part of their community.

- Attend at least one PTA or school function quarterly.

- Never miss a Back to School Night or teacher/parent conference.

- Find validity about the child's needs by obtaining solid data. This might be supplied by regular school testing or individualized psychological and/or educational assessments as required.

- Home responsibilities and chores are important, but should take second place to homework.

- At night, place everything needed for the next day's schoolwork in the child's backpack next to the front door (or back), so it can't be forgotten the next morning.

- Check that the child has homework. If the child is lying about homework, that is still a lie and a serious problem, even if it is a little lie.

- Read to or with a young child every night. Children should see their parents reading at home (even newspapers and magazines convey the importance of reading).

- Directly explain the importance of good grades as a pathway to achievement in obtaining life's long-term rewards.

- Develop a timetable for improved grades.

- Encourage the child to be unafraid to associate with and play with high-achieving children. Parents have a right to express their approval or concern about their child's friends.

- Encourage the child to have extracurricular activities at school. Concentrate on activities that the child actually enjoys to make school a desirable place to be.

- Overall, remember that parents are their child's first and most important teachers. Parenting is a great art, as well as responsibility.

- Parents do play a key role in helping children adjust and master their worlds. This can be particularly challenging when the symptoms of ADHD inhibit practical, functional daily adjustment.

- Parents are to be commended for their efforts, flexibility, perseverance, and creativity in child rearing with kids who present challenges. They need to also realize that they cannot do it all alone and need to network, utilize, and create community supports for their children.

Addressing Homework Issues

Many students with ADHD struggle with homework due to their short attention span, restlessness, and impulsivity. Dr. Arthur Robin (n.d.) stresses the importance of collaboration between parents and teenagers to develop an effective homework structure. This structure should be in place throughout much of the student's academic career and should be adjusted to match the degree of independence that the child can handle. He suggests analyzing the points at which there is a breakdown in the child or adolescents' homework skills using the following set of questions. The family dynamic surrounding homework also should be exam-

ɔte: Although the questions are written for adolescents, they can
ased to identify strengths and weaknesses in children.)

1. Does your adolescent record the assignments in an assignment book, sheet, planner, or in some other organized manner?

2. Does your adolescent bring home from school the assignment books, textbooks, notebooks, and other materials needed to complete homework?

3. Do you review the assignment book and also have an independent means of ensuring that your adolescent is accurately recording the assignments?

4. Does your adolescent select a quiet, non-distracting, well-lit, and comfortable place in which to do the homework?

5. Do you help your teenager develop an organized plan of attack to sequence multiple homework assignments and study in one evening?

6. Have you and your adolescent agreed upon a starting time for doing homework, and does your adolescent adhere to this agreement?

7. Are you or another responsible adult present in the house to "keep your teenager honest" when you expect him or her to be completing homework?

8. Is your adolescent able to sustain his or her attention long enough to complete the homework? Have breaks been built into the plan?

9. Do you review completed written assignments and quiz your adolescent on material studied for examinations?

10. If your adolescent takes stimulant medication, is there an adequate homework dose "on board" during the designated time?

11. Do you coach your adolescent to use a calendar to track long-term assignments and periodically work on them instead of leaving them for the last minute?

12. Does your adolescent have a plan to make sure that the completed assignments actually get to school and are handed in on time?

13. Are there incentives to motivate your adolescent to do homework? (Robin, n.d., ¶1)

Robin (n.d.) suggests the development of a comprehensive homework plan that addresses the weaknesses that have been identified from the above questions. Then he recommends writing this plan down as a behavioral contract and making sure that the parent and the adolescent sign it. Keep in mind to look for improvement, not perfection. It also is important to have incentives specifically identified in the contract. Rewards should occur nightly for following the contract (i.e., a specific amount of time on the phone or watching television), as students like immediate gratification, and also can occur weekly (i.e., a sleepover or a trip to the movies) to ensure commitment to long-term goals.

Robin (n.d.) also suggests implementing the contract for several weeks and then revising it as necessary. He recommends that if there are power struggles with the child or teenager or defiance or resistance, that a psychologist or other mental health professional be consulted for assistance.

According to David Rabiner (n.d.), another helpful technique is to use a "report card" that is taken between home and school each day (see http://www.addresources.org for Rabiner's article and others on homework issues). This simple chart will make it easy to get feedback from the child's teacher about how the child did in the various target areas. As a result, parents are able to reward the child with privileges based on his or her behavior in school.

The following guidelines are suggested for creating and implementing the home-school report card (Rabiner, n.d.):

1. Discuss the plan with your child's teacher. Working together with your child's teacher is important because he or she needs to fill out the ratings each day and it is helpful to create a collaborative relationship with the teacher from the beginning. Discuss with the teacher that you are trying to carefully monitor your child's behavior at school and that this system will give you a lot of information without requiring a lot of his or her time.

2. Decide what target behaviors to include. Input from the teacher is essential in the process. Determine the two or three key areas that you and the teacher think are the most important and where improvement is necessary. Some examples could include completing assigned class work, following class rules, treating peers with respect, and waiting your turn before talking.

3. Decide how to rate your child for each item. Each day your child's teacher will rate your child on the two to three key areas that were chosen in step two. Often parents and teachers like a simple one to five rating scale where 1 indicates a very poor job on the specified behavior, 3 indicates an OK job, and 5 indicates a very good job. See Appendix A for an example of a rating scale.

4. Then construct the daily rating forms (see the example of a rating form in Appendix A and the one provided by Rabiner at http://www.addresources.org/article_adhd_home_school_report_rabiner.php). Supply your child's teacher with these forms so that he or she can complete them each day for your child to bring home.

5. Discuss the plan with your child. It is important that your child understands this plan and is on board with it. Explain that it will provide him the opportunity to earn extra rewards for doing a good job. It is extremely important that your child does not see it as a punishment. The expectations and rewards must be explained clearly from the start. Additionally, it is helpful to ask the teacher to review the ratings each day with your child to make sure your child understands why he or she received the rating. Make sure your child knows what scores he or she needs to earn each day and the target behaviors to earn the agreed upon rewards.

Parents find this system helpful because it provides them with daily feedback from the school about how the child is performing in important areas. Many children also like this system because it provides them with short-term incentives for good behavior. Teachers also are frequently satisfied with this plan because it necessitates very little of their time and makes them feel that their opinion is valued. As a result, there are positive outcomes.

Each morning it is important to make sure that the child knows what she is working on and what is needed to earn the desired reward. It also is important that the child experiences success with this program from the beginning. Otherwise, children and teenagers can quickly become discouraged and lose interest. One way to prevent boredom on the part of the child is to frequently praise her for doing well and initially set up a reward system so that there will be success early on. If the child is unable to earn rewards frequently, she is less likely to work harder. Rotating the rewards according to the child's desires also is helpful in maintaining the child's interest.

A behavioral plan is not a cure for ADHD. Some parents find that their child's behavior is more appropriate while the plan is being implemented, but the unwanted behaviors return once it is discontinued. If assistance is needed in creating a more permanent system of changes to the child's behavior, it often is helpful to consult with a psychologist or other qualified mental health professional.

Advocacy

Some parents choose to hire an advocate who can bring special expertise to the process that provides appropriate educational opportunities for the child with ADHD (Weinfeld & Davis, 2008). According to Weinfeld and Davis (2008), an advocate can help ensure that the student gets the appropriate instruction and services he or she needs. If a parent determines that help negotiating with the child's school is necessary, there are several avenues to choose in order to locate an advocate to consult with about the process of effective collaboration with the school. Options include contacting Children and Adults with Attention Deficit Hyperactivity Disorder (http://www.chadd.org) or the Council of Parent Attorneys and Advocates, Inc. (http://www.

copaa.net) or talking to parents in your community who have already located such services. The book, *Special Needs Advocacy Resource Book,* by Rich Weinfeld and Michelle Davis (2008) also may be helpful.

Parent Information Groups and Parent Training

Many parents find that parent education and support groups help with the initial acceptance of the diagnosis and provide strategies for helping their children manage their symptoms of ADHD. Strategies may focus on difficulties in organization, problem solving, and the management of frustration.

Children and Adults with Attention Deficit Hyperactivity Disorder, often called CHADD, is a national volunteer organization that is very helpful to families of individuals with ADHD. According to its Web site (CHADD, n.d.), each local CHADD affiliate may offer some of the following services:

- free monthly support group meetings,

- special events and conferences,

- local resource information (including a resource table in the back of the meeting room for local advertising of products/services),

- public education and outreach, and

- parent to parent training classes (¶ 1).

Parenting a child with ADHD frequently involves unique challenges. Children with ADHD may respond poorly to typical parenting practices. Because ADHD has a genetic component and runs in families, parents often experience difficulties with organization and consistency themselves and benefit from active assistance in learning parenting skills that are specifically applicable to their child.

Parent training can help parents learn how to appropriately respond to their child's frustrating behaviors and they can learn calm discipline techniques to effectively address these behaviors. Parent-to-parent training is available at many CHADD local chapters. Additionally, some psychologists and other mental health professionals can provide parent training.

chapter 5

The Most Effective Treatment and Management System for ADHD:

The 12-Point Multimodal Action Plan

> "In the power of fixing the attention lies the most precious of the intellectual habits."
> Robert Hall, English clergyman

T H E National Institutes of Mental Health, the American Psychological Association, the National Association of School Psychologists, and other groups emphasize the importance of using a multimodal plan in the diagnosis and treatment of ADHD. This plan includes a combination of medical and behavioral treatment, especially for children with more complex, numerous, and intense symptoms. Additionally, numerous studies from research centers in the U.S., Europe, and Scandinavia recommend a multimodal approach. It has been difficult for parents, educators, and professionals to find a clear model and evolved, comprehensive concept of service delivery. The aim of this chapter and this book is to present an integrated multimodal plan for parents, educators, and professionals to use with individuals with ADHD.

Typical Scenario

Larry is an elementary school student with symptoms of ADHD. He is impulsive, restless, and has trouble paying attention. He calls out in class and engages in seemingly immature "clowning" behaviors that disrupt the classroom. Larry's teacher contacts a parent with a complaint or the parent may contact the teacher for suggestions on how to manage Larry. The child also is referred to the counselor or the school nurse. While the nurse is calling the parent, and then the doctor, Larry breaks a classroom rule and is in the school administrator's office for a discipline complaint.

Communication goes haywire. Larry meets repeated punishment with little consistent follow-up; and a negative self-fulfilling prophecy begins in which Larry develops low self-esteem, but repeats the behavior because it gets some attention. Larry becomes validated by receiving the attention he wants from all parties (albeit negative) and begins to see himself as a "bad" child. He becomes frustrated in school.

Larry's doctor does not return a phone call right away. Everyone looks to the doctor to solve the problem with medicine. When the parents agree to try one form of medication, the doctor sees the child once and issues a prescription based on a brief parent history and observations in the waiting room. The medication may or may not be effective, or the dosage may be too high or too low based on this cursory exam. After little follow-up with the doctor, the family gives up on medication. The school seems more of a place for discipline than a benevolent agent for protecting the child and parties become alienated.

Thus, the child becomes a victim of a system of adults that is really no system at all. Larry's story represents one of the worst-case scenarios, but happens all too frequently.

After seeing so many similar scenarios in clinical practice and educational settings and through years of combined experience, we have found that there are elements that maximize control over the situation, providing a safety net for the child and his self-esteem and greater opportunity for school and life success.

It is important to remember that, for most children affected by ADHD, there is no "cure." ADHD is a lifelong condition that may diminish in severity in some symptom areas with age, but continues to persist into adult life in one form or another. All forms of support are not required throughout the life span. The "tailoring" process for interventions needs to be situationally and developmentally appropriate.

Goldstein (2000) described a comprehensive plan including assessment and treatment, emphasizing how important it is to involve parents and help them take ownership for the process of diagnosis and treatment of their child.

It is our belief that interventions are effective and most powerful when they occur early and are systematic. We believe we have isolated practical interventions that can be conceptualized in 12 components. Take note: This is not a "12-step" program. ADHD is *not* an addiction. The steps are not always sequential or numbered, and they are not all necessary in every example. This plan also is not a "decision tree." The components represent a menu of broad options that can be combined to create helpful solutions. They are to be increasingly based on research as solid studies are brought forward and used artfully based on solid training, experience, and judgment. In a collaborative program where interventions are carefully selected, everyone wins, especially the child.

A 12-Point Multimodal Treatment Plan for Children and Adolescents With ADHD

The following sections present in detail our 12-point multimodal treatment plan for working with children and adolescents with ADHD. The points are as follows:

1. Accurate assessment is utilized.

2. The whole child's strengths are identified and nurtured in the context of unconditional love and acceptance.

3. Parent education on ADHD is provided.

4. Parents participate in training and counseling.

5. Stress is managed.

6. Medical monitoring is provided by a medical professional.

7. The child's diet is reviewed for basic good nutrition.

8. Case management is assigned to a responsible party.

9. Educational supports are provided.

10. A school/home contract is used to monitor schoolwork and homework.

11. Individual and/or group counseling is provided to the child.

12. Calming and relaxation techniques are explored to teach the child how to experience, nurture, and monitor calmness and peacefulness.

1. Accurate Assessment Is Utilized

Many problems parents have in the initial stages of determining if their child has ADHD are due to confusion over diagnosis. Often they seek or are led to medication before the condition is clearly identified properly. Accurate diagnosis is essential, and this process requires various forms of testing. A comprehensive assessment may include testing in the areas of medical, neurological, psychiatric, psychological, neu-ropsychological, social, family systems, educational, and other areas as needed. Appendix B provides further explanation of the assessment and diagnosis process.

Often identification takes place at school. Identification some-times happens through school eligibility committees. Especially for the young child, ADHD may be a part of a broad set of developmental problems. The child and family may be referred to a specialty clinic in a hospital or outpatient practice; educational or other assessments may be recommended; and when broad learning or developmental prob-lems are involved, speech/language assessments and evaluations of motor skills (occupational or physical therapy) may be recommended.

In many mild cases with few, if any, coexisting conditions, a physi-cian's clinical skills may be all that are necessary for going forward with treatment, but often a more comprehensive assessment is required.

Parents often do not anticipate the complexity of a thorough psy-chological assessment, how long it takes, and why it can be so expensive. Psychological assessments generally take 8–17 hours of professional time with about 4–6 hours of direct testing. These assessments can be called *psychological evaluations, clinical psychological evaluations, neurop-sychological evaluations*, or *psychoeducational evaluations*. A school psy-chologist may identify ADHD in many states, although not all states permit DSM-IV diagnoses by a school psychologist, who may not have a doctoral degree. This is not to say that school psychologists lack the competence to make the diagnosis, but that states vary in licensing requirements. Professional clinicians, including psychologists and psy-chiatrists, are capable of conducting private evaluations of your child if you desire, but this process can be costly.

2. The Whole Child's Strengths Are Identified and Nurtured in the Context of Unconditional Love and Acceptance

In addition to diagnosis, assessment data should be used imme-diately to identify strengths and needs with an emphasis on abilities and interests. All adults working with the child are asked to always keep these strengths in mind. A positive tone should be established from the outset to provide children with stability and encouragement as they work on their weaknesses. Some topics covered in guidance to families often contain an assessment of how to use the strengths identified through assessment for appropriate educational and vocational planning, recreational activities, and treatment for comorbid conditions.

Often, by the time the child is identified, he or she is already seen as a "problem." We find that when this mindset is present, children with ADHD begin to see themselves as such. It is quite frequently seen that the child has incorporated a "bad me" self-image like Larry did in our example. At this point the child seeks negative attention to find validation for himself through negative behaviors. A positive view of the child for himself and for his significant others needs to be jump-started early in the game to begin turning around the negative view the child has established in his mind and the minds of others. Anything positive needs to be amplified, including interests, hobbies, and reinforcement preferences.

3. Parent Education Is Provided

Such education can include, but is definitely not limited to, books, films, lecture series, seminars, parent training programs, and association membership. Parents can find learning resources and opportunities by attending local CHADD and similar association meetings, afterschool meetings with a trained professional, or by accessing existing videos or responsible Internet sites. A clinician providing assessment or case management should be able to provide parents with a basic working knowledge of ADHD. There also are some excellent books on the market specifically for parents such as Russell Barkley's (2000b) *Taking Charge of ADHD*.

Demystification is very important, because of all the confusing information parents have been exposed to through the media and Web sites with purely anecdotal supports for trying this or that "cure." There are a number of organizations, Web sites, and parent reference books in the Resources section of this book.

4. Parents Participate in Training and Counseling

Parent training and counseling regarding child management may be required with checkups as needed. An attempt should be made to maximize consistency between significant adults in their philosophy and techniques of child rearing. Parenting stress should be evaluated and the relationship between parenting adults should be examined.

It is very important that the parents have good communication with each other regarding the management of their child with ADHD or suspected ADHD. Although this is good practice in raising all children, this especially is necessary when dealing with a child with a disability. Parents should seek expertise regarding child development, how it is disrupted by ADHD, and how to intervene using teamwork with each other and other stakeholders, such as school personnel. Many parents with very severely disabled children have been seen to communicate beautifully with few problems. On the other hand, parents who communicate poorly and disagree in philosophy and parenting styles can experience great difficulty with children with only mild developmental challenges.

When a sense of teamwork and good communication is found in a parenting couple, a behavior management system can be developed as required. There are a number of parent training programs for this purpose.

Although there are many different parent-training approaches, the parent training section of the MTA study integrated Barkley's (1987) and Forehand and McMahon's (1981) programs into an approach we will detail as one example of a successful parent training program. Anastopoulos, Smith, and Wien (1998) have presented a good overview of the MTA approach. The program was originally designed for a group treatment format but, as utilized in the MTA study, it can be adapted for use with individual families. The program integrates six basic child-management training concepts: (a) consequences need to be immediate, (b) consequences need to be specific, (c) consequences need to be consistent, (d) incentive programs should be established before punishment, (e) parents must anticipate and plan for misbehavior, and (f) family interactions are reciprocal. A more detailed description of these concepts is available in the reprint of Barkley's (1997c) chapter from *Defiant Children: A Clinician's Manual for Parent Training*, available at http://www.guilford.com/excerpts/barkley4EX.html.

There are 10 steps in the program and treatment length is approximately 10 sessions depending on how much of the program is utilized to meet a particular family's needs. It is recommended that that the steps are followed in sequence. Barkley (1997c) clearly delineates the goals, handouts, activities, and homework tasks for each step. The first step concerns reasons why children may exhibit behavior problems including child, parent, and parent-child factors. Parents are taught about the nature of ADHD in this step; providing them with additional ADHD resources (e.g., Barkley, 2000b) may be helpful in that session. The second and third steps focus on improving parental-attending skills and their value to children to increase compliance. Step four introduces a more "formal" reinforcement system involving making privileges contingent on compliance. This is an important intervention for children experiencing ADHD because praise and attention alone often are not enough for them to be successful.

Steps five and six introduce forms of punishment including removal of tokens/points (response cost) and time-out procedures. In step seven, the skills that parents have learned are applied to managing their children's behavior in public places. The daily school-home behavior report card is discussed in step eight. The child's behavior is reinforced with points at school and then rewarded at home. This intervention potentially can significantly impact not only the child's behavior in school but also school-home relationships and parent-child relationships. A common experience for the parent of a child with ADHD is that any contact from the school means that their child has not been successful in some way at school (i.e., "any news is bad news"). The school-home behavior report card changes the contingencies so that the child and parent are learning about the child daily regardless of his or her behavior. Step nine concerns preparing to handle behaviors that the child might exhibit in the future and hence functions as sort of a relapse prevention session, except that the behaviors have not yet occurred. Finally, the last step is a one-month support session.

If a child has significant behavioral problems, it is likely that the school has suggested or developed a Functional Behavior Assessment and Behavior Intervention Plan for that child. It is important that both home and school plans are properly integrated with each other, with similar language, contingencies, and consequences. Some clinics offer behavior training in the home as an outreach service.

Clinically, it is very helpful to break down the child's entire day into 15-minute segments to see that there is both balance of quality of life and structure and control where it is needed. Parents can identify stress points in the child's day where a plan needs to be shored up.

5. Stress Is Managed

Parents need to identify symptoms of their own stress, evaluate the effects of strain on their marriage, and seek respite for one another. Stress reduction techniques should be selected and employed by parents, including relaxation opportunities and changes in routines or environment. Personalized informal stress-checking (such as taking a moment to breathe deeply and evaluate a situation) is important for parents, teachers, and administrators. Adults need to strive to be calm islands in the lives of children who are experiencing disruption or dysregulation in their own nervous systems. Adults need to model calmness, an experience that many children with ADHD have not witnessed or experienced. The pressure from impulsive and, sometimes, oppositional behavior and the conflicting messages of adult stakeholders in a disorganized system can compromise the objectiveness required for the situation.

6. Medical Monitoring Is Provided by Medical Personnel

Medical monitoring regarding the kind of and level of prescription medication (if prescribed) should be provided by medical personnel. This is the area that gives parents and kids the most difficulty or trepidation. Research has clearly demonstrated that it can be the most effective intervention and, often, a standalone one (based on the MTA study results). When medications are prescribed, they should be fully explained along with a discussion of possible side effects. It is very important that as many members of the treatment group, including the child, buy into the program. This includes following through on taking medications as prescribed. See Chapter 3 for comprehensive consideration of all of the factors involved in medical intervention for ADHD.

7. The Child's Diet Is Reviewed for Basic Good Nutrition

It is clear that, in some extreme cases, poor diet can result in behavioral symptoms that appear to be identical to ADHD. Of course, a hungry child also can be an inattentive, depressed, and angry child. Hunger can be due to poor nutrition as much as it can be due to low volumes of food. A balanced, healthy diet is a requisite for development and learning. There are few if any scientifically proven dietary interventions with research-based evidence of effectiveness. Chapter 10, which focuses on alternative treatments, will be helpful when considering dietary changes for the child with ADHD. We are not suggesting that poor diet alone always engenders ADHD symptoms, but poor diet can be part of a lifestyle of too much passive entertainment (e.g., video games, television, etc), lack of recreation, and inadequate supervision or structure that can increase the symptoms of ADHD.

8. Case Management Is Assigned to a Responsible Party

Case management should be assigned to a responsible party, such as a parent, therapist, school counselor, special educator, or school nurse. Case managers communicate with all relevant parties regarding medications and preplanned intervention strategies.

Goldstein (2000) reports that, in his experience, a pediatrician or family practitioner can medically manage at least half of all children with properly diagnosed ADHD efficiently. Approximately 30% of children with ADHD should seek psychiatric consultation due to co-occurring problems to assist in the choice and titration of medication. Their primary care physician can then manage these children. Finally, a child psychiatrist should closely follow approximately 20% of children with ADHD with more significant and multiple problems.

Most frequently, the parents act as case managers. For some busy parents, school officials or the school nurse may act as case managers. It is important that the lines of communication stay open and are consistent within the framework of a real, and preferably, written plan.

The case manager should be viewed as the primary communication conduit. When communicating with busy medical or educational staff, parents may wish to find agreeable times and/or conduits for communication (i.e., e-mail). Playing "telephone tag" through voicemails often impedes communication between parties, so written communication such as e-mails provides both convenience and assurance that messages are delivered properly.

9. Educational Supports Are Provided

Educational interventions should be provided for the child to ensure that he or she is receiving a free appropriate education as required by special education law. Our instructional chapter (Chapter 6) addresses the following areas of educational support:

- adaptations,
- the need for a Section 504 Plan or IEP under IDEA,

- advocacy issues,

- special education placement,

- accommodations for instruction and testing,

- teaching strategies, and

- participation in a case-managed home/school plan.

Teaching strategies must take into account classroom management, class environment factors, and teaching techniques appropriate for the child. The child with ADHD requires a school day that is tailored to circumvent, alleviate, remediate, or at least improve the time he or she is on task. The concept of engaged learning, or engaged time on task, is central in conceptualizing how much time the child actually accesses instruction. Children with ADHD rarely find themselves actively engaged in instruction to the same degree as children without the disorder. Their access to instruction needs to be facilitated by specific instructional strategies as contained in Chapter 6, which discusses teaching strategies. Some programs try to train attention through exercises, like listening to tapes. This particularly is the case when addressing the needs of adults with ADHD, who might be able to exercise greater cognitive control in extending their listening skills. Some of these techniques are covered in our technology section in Chapter 9. For educational purposes, attentional training in the classroom is rarely a viable activity, given curricular time restraints.

Teacher training is, of course, important. There is a great deal of need for flexibility and the ability to ignore behaviors at times in order to reward positive accomplishments. Greene (1995) conducted a thorough study in which teacher factors were reviewed, emphasizing the importance of teacher characteristics and the need for stability between relationships of all adults involved.

It also is best to plan or structure the summer activities of children and teens with ADHD. A number of summer camp programs are available, some of which have research-based activities effective for students with ADHD. Selection of a summer program or camp needs to be a good fit for your child. Learn about the philosophy of the program, the training of the staff (or at least the management), and the actual activities provided. Pelham, Wheeler, and Chronis (1998) demonstrated that intensive peer-focused behavioral interventions could be successfully implemented in recreational settings. The majority of children with ADHD, however, may not require a special summer program, but they do not benefit from being idle in the summers. Because of their need for structure, children with ADHD need organized summer activities. In this case, parents may want to look at extracurricular activities such as sports, art programs, or college classes for adolescents. Parents should always communicate their child's strengths and weaknesses to summer program directors, teachers, and coaches. Some local chapters of ADHD organizations can aid parents in finding good summer opportunities for their children.

10. A School/Home Contract Is Used to Monitor Schoolwork and Homework

A daily or weekly class-by-class monitoring sheet may be necessary with home consequences for compliance. Classwork, homework, and organizational skill objectives may be identified as requirements for each subject. Effectiveness of strategies can be monitored through periodic teacher and parent ratings of attention, activity level, and related personality/behavior variables. This is the most important aspect of case management and warrants its own emphasis, because this is where reinforcement through consistency contingent on child behavior is delivered. This may involve a "daily report card" (see Appendix A) or other form of regular communication between home and school. Home/school communication works effectively, as demonstrated by research by Murray, Rabiner, Schulte, and Newitt (2008), who evaluated a Daily Report Card (DRC). Intervention participants demonstrated significant improvement in academic skills and productivity during post-test studies as compared to control participants, with moderately large effect sizes, which were sustained over a 4-month period (Murray et al., 2008). Teacher and student buy-in to long-term intervention success also is important in increasing school success (Finn & Sladeczek, 2001).

11. Individual and/or Group Counseling Is Provided to the Child

Individual and/or group counseling for the child should focus on self-evaluation, self-monitoring, and educational self-advocacy. Peer relations and self-esteem issues also should be addressed. Research data does not suggest that group counseling or therapy cures or even alleviates the core symptoms of ADHD. Dr. Stanley Fagen (personal communication, October 2008) has conducted groups for children with ADHD for more than 13 years. His observations support the findings in the literature that there are many aspects of child development and mental health that can be improved in such groups, even if core symptoms of ADHD such as inattention, impulse control, or restlessness are not notably changed through such participation. He emphasizes the progress that can be made in self-esteem through working with other children and in accepting their strengths and weaknesses.

12. Calming and Relaxation Techniques Are Explored to Teach the Child How to Experience, Nurture, and Monitor Calmness and Peacefulness

Many children have no experience of feeling calm or being centered or at peace. The potential for peace is a revelation to persons who have never experienced it. A calm base often is an unexpressed goal for most of us. It partly explains why we seek beachfront, mountain, and cruise vacations. We also seek a mental state where there is at least a temporary cessation of rumination, distraction, and anxiety. To some extent these states can be induced by age-old practices of meditation and mindfulness or modern-day systems of relaxation therapy. Calming exercises, including yoga and meditation, may be valuable techniques that might be incorporated into life as children develop and gain some improvement in self-control. The feeling of calmness may generalize as children grow accustomed to understanding what it means and feels like. These approaches need to be applied with some frequency, because they have yet to be demonstrated to produce permanent changes in the brain or in chemistry on their own. See Chapter 10 on alternative treatments for further exploration of this point.

Where Can An ADHD Multimodal Plan Be Found or Established?

A multimodal ADHD plan can be found or established with case management at a school. Increasingly, school counselors manage 504 Plans, while a school special education teacher or school supervisor of special education services will manage IEPs. Case management also is supplied by consultation from a school psychologist or school social worker.

Multimodal type ADHD clinics are also found in private practices. Many private practices have psychologists, psychiatrists, social workers, psychiatric nurses, marriage and family therapists, licensed professional counselors, and other licensed mental health specialists under one roof. Such practices may have an ADHD "subspecialty" practice as a separate division.

ADHD clinics also are found in hospitals, especially children's hospitals, university hospitals, and university departments of psychiatry or psychology. These are sometimes used as training opportunities for graduate students. Many public health departments have clinics and might have a monthly "open house" for patients with ADHD, for example.

Do Multimodal Plans Work?

MTA subject groups were evaluated in studies at 9, 14, and 24 months after the original study by Jensen et al. (2005). The MTA medication strategy showed persisting significant superiority over behavior and community care for ADHD and oppositional-defiant symptoms at 24 months, although not as great as at 14 months. Significant additional benefits of combined care over medication management and of behavior over community care were not found for core ADHD symptoms. However, the multimodal, combined treatment was consistently superior for anxiety symptoms, academic performance, oppositional behaviors, parent-child relations, and social skills. The researchers concluded that the benefits of intensive medication management for ADHD extend 10 months beyond the intensive treatment phase only in core symptoms and diminish over time. The multimodal, combined treatment was more effective in these domains than the routine community care and the single treatments of medication only or behavioral treatment only. Arnold et al. (2004) examined 9-month data from the MTA study as a further check on the relative effect of medication and behavioral treatment. After the behavioral treatment had been completely faded out, medication and the combination of medication and behavioral treatment were found to be significantly superior to just behavior treatment and community care for ADHD and oppositional-defiant (ODD) symptoms, with mixed results for social skills and internalizing symptoms.

In a research forum on psychological treatment of adults with ADHD by Weiss et al. (2008), a literature search found five empirical studies of psychological treatment for adults with ADHD out of 1,419 articles on ADHD in adults. Practice guidelines to date all recommend multimodal intervention, given that a significant number of subjects could not tolerate, did not respond to, or failed to reach optimal outcomes with medication alone in adulthood. The researchers found that studies of brief, structured, and short-term psychological interventions for adults with ADHD demonstrated moderate to large effect sizes. Methodological problems were noted in many studies. The researchers reported that psychological treatment might play a critical role in the management of adults with ADHD who are motivated and developmentally ready to acquire new skills as symptoms remit.

Symptom Improvement

Recently, Toplak, Connors, Shuster, Knezevic, and Parks (2008) have visited some of these issues in their review of cognitive, cognitive-behavioral, and neural-based interventions for ADHD. In the review, controlling for medication status was found to be very important to determine whether effects are attributable to medication or an interaction between treatment and medication.

Again, while core symptoms of ADHD are not always improved, there has been some evidence to demonstrate effectiveness of cognitive strategies combined with behavioral programs applied to specific domains, such as social skills and anger management, as the Toplak group point out. Toplak et al. (2008) state, "More consideration should be given to an integrated approach to intervention that addresses cognitive, motivational, and family and school contexts (Hinshaw, 2006), as children likely experience their symptoms in multiple contexts, and therefore need treatment in each setting to obtain maximal benefit" (p. 19).

Academic Improvement From Non-Pharmacological Interventions

Recently, Trout, Ortiz Lienemann, Reed, and Epstein (2007) examined 41 studies that evaluated the impact of nonmedication interventions on the academic functioning of students with ADHD. "The findings revealed that a broad range of traditional and nontraditional interventions has been used to improve students' academic outcomes, yet systematic lines of research were clearly missing" (Trout et al., 2007, p. 207).

The studies mostly focused on children who underachieve because of ADHD. For example, according to Trout et al. (2007) studies evaluating underachievement of children with ADHD have found that up to 80% of these children experience academic performance or learning problems. In addition, more than half of them may require academic tutoring of some form, and studies found that between 40% and 50% of underachieving children also identified as having ADHD eventually will receive services in special education programs. Overall, Trout et al. found studies showing that achievement test scores of children with ADHD frequently fall below those of typical peers on core academic subjects, such as reading, spelling, and math.

Because of the chronic nature of ADHD, the risk of academic failure is likely to remain as children reach adolescence. Between 70% and 80% of children with ADHD continue to display symptoms of impulsivity and inattention into adolescence to a degree considered inappropriate for their age (Barkley, 1998). Furthermore, the academic outcomes of students with ADHD reveal that adolescents in this population are more likely to be retained, drop out, or get suspended from school, and are less likely to continue on to postsecondary education (Barkley, Fischer, Edelbrock, & Smallish, 1990; Klein & Manuzza 1991; Weiss & Hechtman, 1993).

Currently, the most common intervention strategy used with children with ADHD is psychostimulant medication. School-based interventions are seen less frequently in the research. The most recent meta-analysis of school-based interventions examined both behavioral and academic outcomes over a 24-year period, from 1971 to 1995 (DuPaul & Eckert, 1997). Of the 63 studies reviewed, only 8 addressed academic outcomes exclusively. DuPaul and Eckert (1998) further examined the literature from 1971 to 1995 and, after including unpublished reports, were still only able to identify 15 studies addressing academic outcomes. Conclusions from their review revealed many weaknesses in the research. Trout et al. (2007) were unable to locate any more current evaluations of the literature on academic interventions for school-age populations with ADHD, and no reviews have looked exclusively at the nonmedical interventions used to improve the academic outcomes of children with ADHD.

Trout et al. (2007), citing Weiss and Hechtman (1993) conclude that medication has limitations; specifically, almost one fourth of children with ADHD do not respond favorably to medication. In addition, they point out that limitations extend to educators, who have little control over medication levels prescribed to students, the administration of the drugs, or adherence to medication schedules. Because of these conclusions, Trout et al. state that effective, nonmedication treatment strategies are imperative to improving academic success and suggest that, given the number of children with ADHD and the potentially serious long-term consequences of the academic failure of these children, more research attention should be paid to using nonmedical interventions with children with ADHD, particularly in regard to their education.

What Are the Effects of Multimodal Treatment on Coexisting Symptoms?

Hechtman et al. (2005) attempted to answer the question, "Does multimodal treatment of ADHD decrease other diagnoses?" They examined the persistence and development of conditions other than ADHD, such as oppositional defiant disorder (ODD), conduct disorder (CD), anxiety, depression, and learning disabilities (LD) in the MTA study data set. Only the combined group was significantly better than the community care group in reducing total number of disorders and impairment at 14 months in subjects with multiple conditions at baseline. Well-titrated and monitored stimulant medication can decrease ODD and possibly prevent future CD, the researchers concluded. Combined treatment may be required for the most disturbed children with ADHD who have multiple disorders and severe impairment. So, again, it appears that medication cannot only affect core symptoms of ADHD, but may decrease oppositional symptoms. Combined multimodal treatment may be most effective with children with multiple coexisting conditions.

Aren't Multimodal Programs More Time Consuming and Costly, Especially in Today's World of Skyrocketing Insurance Costs?

Jensen et al. (2005) reported that multimodal treatment is more costly than single interventions. Medication management was the least expensive, followed by behavioral treatment, and then combined treatment. Lower costs of medication treatment were found in the community care group, reflecting the less intensive (and less effective) nature of community-delivered treatment. Medical management was more effective but more costly than community care and more cost-effective than combination treatment and behavioral treatment alone. Under some conditions, combination treatment (medical management and psychotherapy) was somewhat more cost-effective, as demonstrated by lower costs per additional child "normalized," among children with multiple comorbid disorders. Jensen et al. concluded that medical management treatment, although not as effective as combined medical management and behavioral treatment, is likely to be more cost-effective in routine treatment for children with ADHD, particularly those without comorbid disorders. For some children with comorbid disorders, it may be cost-effective to provide combination treatment. When we consider the long-term social costs of ADHD upon society, a thorough early intervention approach may be more costly initially but pay great dividends in the long run.

Peer Relationships

Peer relationships were studied by Hoza, Mrug, Pelham, Greiner, & Gnagy (2003). Peer-assessed outcomes were examined at the end of treatment (14 months after study entry) for 285 children (226 boys, 59 girls) who were rated by their classmates (2,232 classmates total) using peer sociometric procedures. All children with ADHD were participants in the MTA study. Results indicated that children from all groups remained significantly impaired in their peer relationships. Peer relationships can improve, however, through individual and group therapy treatment, although this has been demonstrated clinically and not through hard research. These effects depend on highly targeted therapeutic strategies and direct social skill instruction that cannot be quantified or replicated through an "off-the-shelf" treatment program.

Ethnicity and Efficacy of Treatment

The effects of ethnicity on treatment in the 14-month outcome study were reported by Arnold et al. (2003). From the MTA study the authors matched each African American and Latino participant with randomly selected White participants of same sex, treatment group, and site. Although White children were significantly less symptomatic than African American and Latino children on some ratings, response to treatment did not differ significantly by ethnicity after controlling for public assistance. Ethnic minority families cooperated with and benefited significantly from combination (multimodal) treatment (compared with medication). This incremental gain withstood statistical control for mother's education, single-parent status, and public assistance. Treatment for lower socioeconomic status minority children, especially if they have other disorders, should combine medication and behavioral treatment.

These findings are important. The lack of universal health care at this writing can result in the absence of adequate attention to children with ADHD brought to medical attention and the lack of clinical follow-up with a comprehensive plan. Although the benefits of comprehensive care are important in the long run, assessments and repeated treatment visits can be very expensive to the uninsured in the short run.

Preschool

There has been much controversy over early identification and inclusion of preschool children in diagnosis and the overprescription of medication to younger children. McGoey, Eckert, and DuPaul (2002) provide a very systematic and thorough literature review of early intervention for preschool-age children with ADHD. They concluded that three primary treatment approaches (stimulant medication, parent training, and classroom behavior management) were effective in reducing symptoms of ADHD in young children, although few of the studies focused on preschool children in particular. They were able to find only 14 studies of nonpharmacological approaches to reducing inattentiveness, impulsivity, and hyperactivity in young children. They noted that some professionals are hesitant to medicate young children who have ADHD, instead recommending parent training and behavior interventions, but they were able to find only one published study examining the use of multimodal treatments with young children with ADHD. Although they found results of this study to be positive, only six children were included in the study and it did not examine long-term outcomes, posing clear issues regarding the effectiveness of the study. McGoey et al. recommended a longitudinal multicomponent analysis of treatment to delineate an optimal approach for working with young children who have ADHD.

An Example of an Action Plan

Foy and Earls (2005) described a plan of pediatrician involvement in community care of ADHD, noting that large discrepancies between pediatricians' practice patterns and the American Academy of Pediatrics guidelines for assessing and treating children with ADHD still exist. The authors raised concerns about access to ADHD treatment for girls, minorities, and poorer individuals, and stated that community collaboration in care is crucial to improving clinical practice, especially collaborations with school. Such collaboration, Foy and Earls suggested, addresses other barriers to good care, such as parental and school pressure to prescribe medications, cultural biases that may prevent schools from assessing children for ADHD or families from seeking health care, and inconsistencies in recognition of ADHD and referral for services among schools in the same district or school system. Collaboration also aids communication, especially data collection, they noted.

Foy and Earls (2005) focused on a program in Guilford County, NC, that sought to develop a consensus among health care providers, educators, and child advocates regarding the assessment and treatment of children with symptoms of ADHD. The article described one protocol used by school personnel and community physicians for more than 10 years that ensured communication and collaboration between educators and physicians in the assessment and treatment of children with symptoms of ADHD.

Perhaps most importantly, the community process through which the protocol was developed and implemented had an educational component that increased the knowledge of school personnel about ADHD and its treatment, thus increasing the likelihood that referrals would be appropriate and that children would benefit from coordination of interventions among school personnel, physicians, and parents. The protocol reflected a consensus of school personnel and community health care providers regarding the following (Foy & Earls, 2005):

1. ideal ADHD assessment and management principles;

2. a common entry point (a team) at schools for children needing assessment because of inattention and classroom behavior problems, whether the problems present first to a medical provider, the behavioral health system, or the school;

3. a protocol followed by the school system that recognized the school's resource limitations but met the needs of community health care providers for classroom observations, psychoeducational testing, parent and teacher behavior rating scales, and functional assessment;

4. a packet of information about each child who is determined to need medical assessment and a contact person or team at each physician's office to receive the packet from the school and direct it to the appropriate clinician;

5. an assessment process that investigated comorbidities and applied appropriate diagnostic criteria;

6. evidence-based interventions;

7. processes for follow-up monitoring of children after establishment of a treatment plan; roles for central participants (school personnel, physicians, school nurses, and mental health professionals) in assessment, management, and follow-up monitoring of children with attention problems;

8. forms for collecting and exchanging information at every step;

9. processes and key contacts for flow of communication at every step; and

10. a plan for educating school and health care professionals about the new processes. (p. E97)

The description of the successful North Carolina program by Foy and Earls (2005) can and should be used by other communities to implement effective planning and programming for meeting the education needs of children with ADHD. Parents can suggest similar plans to their child's pediatricians and school staff members in order to improve collaboration and communication between all parties.

Universality of Findings

Döpfner et al. (2004) researched effectiveness of a multimodal treatment program in Europe. Children with ADHD were assigned to either behavior therapy (including continued psychoeducation) or medical management with methylphenidate plus psychoeducation.

Depending on the effectiveness, the treatment was either terminated, if totally effective, with long-term aftercare and continuation of medication if needed; if partially effective, the other treatment component was added (combined treatment); or if ineffective, the treatment components were replaced. Thus, a treatment rationale was applied that resulted in an adaptive and individually tailored therapy—similar to a strategy that may be useful in clinical practice. ADHD symptoms, behavior problems and comorbid symptoms were significantly reduced during the course of treatment. Teacher ratings reported that combined treatment was more effective than behavior therapy. Döpfner et al. concluded that both behavior therapy and combined treatment are effective interventions within an individually tailored multimodal treatment strategy.

In the Netherlands, Van den Hoofdakker et al. (2007), investigated the effectiveness of behavioral parent training (BPT) as an adjunct to routine clinical care. Adjunctive BPT was found to enhance the effectiveness of routine treatment of children with ADHD, particularly in decreasing behavioral and internalizing problems, but not in reducing ADHD symptoms or parenting stress. Furthermore, adjunctive BPT may limit the prescription of polypharmaceutical treatment.

The Most Preferred Treatment Method

Overall, it seems that a family-based, behaviorally oriented, multimodal, and multisystem approach is currently the most preferred treatment for children with ADHD, especially where there are coexisting conditions. Specifically, multimodal behavioral treatments involving the family and school, in conjunction with medication, is most advantageous for some age groups, particularly latency-age children (7 to 10 years old) experiencing ADHD combined type. The treatment approach must involve family and school environments. Several researchers in the field (e.g., Barkley, 1998) have recommended this type of treatment package prior to the MTA study, but the MTA study has been very important in providing a structure for further, refined research and in providing very provocative and informative initial findings that inform treatment.

chapter 6

Strategies Used by Successful Teachers for Children With Attentional Issues

> "Attention makes the genius; all learning, fancy, and science depend upon it. Newton traced back his discoveries to its unwearied employment. It builds bridges, opens new worlds, and heals diseases; without it taste is useless, and the beauties of literature are unobserved."
> Robert Aris Willmott, English author

ALTHOUGH it is among the most noble and often most satisfying professions, teaching can be an overwhelming job. In most general education classrooms, the teacher has a broad spectrum of learners. Educators are responsible for analyzing, knowing, and understanding each individual student's strengths, interests, and needs. They are responsible for knowing their school system's and individual school's policies and procedures, national standards, curriculum demands and requirements, educational theory, assorted instructional strategies, resources and materials, psychology, and child development. When teachers have students with ADHD in their classrooms, they are further responsible for knowing and understanding the 2004 reauthorization of the federal Individuals with Disabilities Education Act (IDEA), Section 504, and the Responsiveness to Intervention (RTI) approach, used by some schools to evaluate students with learning disabilities, because they can and do affect school practices (Jeweler, Barnes-Robinson, Roffman Shevitz, & Weinfeld, 2008).

The majority of individuals with ADHD experience problems with school performance (see http://www.russellbarkley.org for more information on how these problems can manifest). As many as 30%–50% of students with ADHD are retained in their school grade at least once; 25%–36% never complete high school (Barkley, n.d.). In the face of all of these challenges, excellent teachers learn and practice strategies that help students with ADHD become successful learners. The following sections provide best practices that have been proven to work successfully in classrooms that include children with ADHD (many of these also work well with students who do not have ADHD). A scenario is continued in these sections to demonstrate how one teacher might implement the best practices in his or her classroom. Parents can use these best practices as a guide to helping them understand their child's education and work with his or her teacher to ensure that the instructor has all of the information and support needed to help the child succeed.

Best Practice 1: Knowledge Is Power!

Prior to the opening of the new school year, Ms. R. joined her colleagues at the professional development meeting scheduled to review information about her incoming fifth-grade students. She was joined by her grade level team, the school counselor, and the speech and language therapist. Ms. R. had already received the index cards prepared by the students' previous year's teacher with the important academic, medical, social, and behavioral notes on each student. A roundtable discussion ensued regarding the strengths and needs of each student and the programs and services that would be provided. In addition, Ms. R. rounded out the picture of each student by reviewing his or her cumulative records and the confidential records of children with disabilities. She and the school counselor had already met with the parents of children with disabilities during the August teacher preparation week.

Gathering data about a child is imperative. The more a teacher knows and understands about a student, the better able she is to plan, prepare, and practice strategies that will work best for each student. Written records and staff input, including from teachers in the arts and specialists, help to create a more complete student profile. In this respect it is very important to accurately keep and maintain records. Index cards are helpful for doing so, and teachers should be prepared to document the strengths and needs of their students, especially those with ADHD and other disabilities. Such documentation only aides future teachers in providing accommodations students need. Parents also should maintain orderly and accurate records, keeping copies of letters and other materials (including report cards and progress reports) sent home. By law, parents are eligible to receive copies of student records held by school districts. Parents may wish to periodically request copies of student records for their personal files. If the educator does not have accurate information from the student's previous teachers, he or she may wish to contact the parents, advocate, or case manager to learn as much about a child as possible.

Best Practice 2: Create an Environment of Mutual Respect, Acceptance, Organization, Flexibility, and High Expectations

As each student entered Ms. R's classroom, she greeted him or her with a smile and a few words. As the result of a full group discussion, classroom rules and standards were created and clearly posted on the board and on one of the many colorful information stations on the walls. These rules reflected the academic, behavior, and social goals agreed upon by the class. Ms. R. explained the organization of her classroom including the typical schedule, the routines, the open lines of communication, and her expectations for a successful year.

At the beginning of the school year, the teacher sets the climate for collaboration, caring, respect, and negotiation for the year. Good classrooms become places where risk-taking is encouraged and making mistakes is the way one grows and learns. The environment in such classrooms is not competitive, but rather a place where students measure their progress internally, and receive a sense of worth and accomplishment from within. Student strengths are recognized and rewarded early and regularly. The teacher models a sense of unconditional acceptance and responsibility.

Classroom rules should be established by the students in a spirit of fairness and an appreciation and valuing of individual differences. The rules should be posted in a prominent place and always referred to when problems arise. Problem-solving processes need to be formally taught and practiced throughout the year, and students should be expected to apply them as needed. Students should use these skills in their relationships in school, as well as be able to recognize when these skills are used in literature, history, and social studies. These skills have real-world applications and consequences. Many successful classrooms have a suggestion box where students are encouraged to share ideas to improve the sense of community in the classroom.

Classroom organization must be flexible, yet structured with opportunities for collaborative goal setting, significant peer interactions, and cooperative learning. Students should be immersed in a climate that promotes self-efficacy and a solid sense of self-sufficiency while being provided with instruction that demands the use of their abilities. By maintaining high expectations and standards in an atmosphere of support, humor, and comfort, teachers help students grow academically and love learning (Weinfeld, Barnes-Robinson, Jeweler, & Roffman Shevitz, 2006).

Best Practice 3: Provide Strength-Based Instruction

Sammy, one of Ms. R's students, is diagnosed with ADHD and has an IEP. After reviewing all of the school information regarding Sammy, she began to analyze the implications for instruction. Through an Interest Survey, a student conference, informal and formal diagnostic testing, careful observation, staff input, parent input, and contact with Sammy's pediatrician and psychologist, Ms. R. was able to carefully plan appropriate instruction. She recognized Sammy's strengths, interests, talents, learning style, and his needs regarding attentional issues.

Sammy is a bright child who is strong in the visual-spatial area and a hands-on learner. Ms. R. learned that Sammy has a good long-term visual memory, sees relationships, thinks primarily in pictures, learns complex concepts easily, is creative and intuitive, has a sophisticated sense of humor, is better at math reasoning, and loves to build and construct with a variety of materials (Ricci, Barnes-Robinson, & Jeweler, 2006).

Sammy's attention issues result in the following: lack of attention to detail on written work, missing important verbal and non-verbal cues, poor planning for assignments, making many careless errors, and missing deadlines.

Research and a review of successful programs indicate that the most important component of the education of these students is providing instruction in the student's area of strength. Working through a child's strengths puts a positive spin on learning, especially for a student who has had continued difficulty in school (Weinfeld et al., 2006). In addition, encouraging a student's strengths builds self-confidence in his or her ability to learn material. For example, an assignment that asks a student to build a Web page on the difference between frogs and toads in lieu of a traditional report could connect a student's strength in technology with new material being taught in the classroom, in this case, amphibians. Teachers also can implement a student's strengths in a particular area by allowing him or her to serve as an expert on the topic or method. Some students delight in being given new responsibilities connected to their strengths, especially if they previously were given instruction that only addressed their weaknesses. Such emphasis on strengths can be accomplished by differentiating instruction, a classroom tool recommended for use with all students and described in the next section.

Best Practice 4: Differentiate Instruction

Ms. R., working with Sammy's case manager and using his IEP, gives Sammy preferential seating, uses manipulatives in math, and incorporates visual aids like graphic organizers or diagrams with Sammy. She gives him highlighters to focus on key words and ideas and provides hands-on activities that capture his attention. She provides a color-coded assignment book to write down all of his assignments that they will check each day in order to address his attention issues. She provides opportunities for classroom computer access and assistive technology whenever needed. Ms. R., recognizing his visual-spatial skills and interests, allows him to do alternative products that reflect his clear understanding of concepts and content material.

When differentiated, instruction better matches an individual's abilities, styles, and needs. Differentiation is a way of thinking about and planning instruction in order to meet the diverse needs of students based on their characteristics. Teachers differentiate content, process, and product according to students' readiness, interest, and learning profiles through a range of instructional and management strategies (Renzulli, 1977; Tomlinson, 1999).

Content is the subject matter prescribed by the state or district program of studies. For example, in social studies, students may be asked to write a research paper on the Civil War. *Process* is the internalization of information. Following the steps for the paper from notes, to outline, to draft illustrates a process a student follows when dealing with the content material. Some children with ADHD may need to break the tasks into smaller parts and have check-in points with the teacher. *Product* is the outcome of the application of the process to the content. The finished research paper is the product. Providing differentiation for these students, a variety of resources could be used to study the Civil War (content); organizational software and assisted note-taking may aid in internalizing information (process); and the student may demonstrate his or her understanding through a model, dramatization, or PowerPoint presentation (product; Weinfeld et al., 2006).

The following are examples of specific ways to differentiate instruction in each of the three categories (Tomlinson, 1999):

Content

- Use multiple texts
- Use varied resources
- Compact curriculum
- Provide learning contracts

Process

- Use interactive journals
- Use tiered assignments
- Create interest centers
- Create learning centers

Product

- Provide varied modes of expression, materials, technologies

- Implement advanced assignments that require higher order thinking skills
- Provide authentic assessment
- Use self- and peer-evaluations

Best Practice 5: Provide Appropriate Interventions, Adaptations, and Accommodations

Ms. R. meets with Sammy and his parents to discuss his IEP goals and the adaptations and accommodations he will be receiving in class. They discuss Sammy's strengths and needs. His counselor, the school psychologist, and a special education resource teacher might choose to attend this meeting. A case manager on the team will be established—Ms. R. or a special education teacher—and a regular channel of communication will be established (his parents prefer to communicate with his case manager and school staff through e-mail). They agree on specific days of the week and best times in case a voice conference is required.

They work out the signals that will act as cues to Sammy to listen to directions. In addition, they plan on ways to help Sammy pay attention to details in his written work. A task analysis and calendar are set up for each major assignment. In order to tap into Sammy's interest in building, a mentor, who is an architect, has been contacted to work with Sammy on a one-to-one project. Sammy also will join a "lunch bunch" with the school counselor to reinforce strategies that address his attentional issues.

Evaluation is an important component when providing appropriate adaptations and accommodations. Ms. R. sets up conferences with Sammy about his progress on his goals. A daily assignment sheet is signed by the teacher for accuracy, sent home with Sammy each day, and is returned the next day with a parent signature. He and his parents will agree to the plan, and a system of rewards will be established at home for positive behavior and progress on his goals at school. Ms. R. is diligent about positive reinforcement and support.

As Sammy shows improvement, a goal may be adjusted or dropped. However, Ms. R recognizes that ongoing evaluation is essential.

When it is suspected that a student has ADHD, it is crucial that the adults who are involved come together with the student to analyze the student's strengths and needs and then jointly create an appropriate intervention plan. Next, the current program should be evaluated to see how well it is nurturing and developing the student's strengths, while adapting and accommodating for the weaknesses. Finally, recommendations should be made for program changes that will result in the appropriate level of challenge and the instruction and support that will develop the student's strengths and strengthen his weaknesses.

Once a student's abilities and challenges have been explored, educators should take a close look at the current program to see how well it is addressing both the identified strengths and challenges and examine what rigorous programming already is in place to address the student's strengths. Next, teachers can explore the variety of supports, interventions, and instruction that are in place to both circumvent weaknesses and provide opportunities for strengthening them. They should analyze the adaptations and accommodations that are currently in place and look at the special instruction in which the student is participating. We also recommend that educators look at the special behavior management plans and counseling that are in place to meet the student's behavioral needs. Finally, teachers should look at the case management practices to ensure that all pieces are being addressed appropriately and that there is effective communication between and among all staff and parents.

After completing a thorough analysis of the student's strengths and weaknesses and the current instruction and interventions that are in place, recommendations can be made for adjustments in the student's program. These recommendations become the intervention plan that helps each student reach his or her potential. The intervention plan includes recommendations for the special instruction, behavioral/attention plans, and counseling support that the student needs. The intervention plan specifies who is responsible for the case management and ensures that all staff and parents are functioning as a team to successfully implement the intervention plan. Finally, the intervention plan specifies how things will be implemented and who is responsible for implementation.

Many accommodations allow students with learning challenges to demonstrate their knowledge without being handicapped by the effects of their difficulties. In planning, it is crucial that the teacher consider instructional methods and strategies that either circumvent the student's difficulties or build in the necessary scaffolding to empower students to be successful with the demands of the assignment.

When advocating for adaptations and accommodations, it is essential for educators, parents, and students to first understand the differences between an adaptation and an accommodation. These definitions will help:

- *Accommodation:* Procedure or enhancement that empowers a person with a disability to complete a task that he or she would otherwise be unable to complete because of his or her disability (Maryland State Department of Education, 1999).

- *Adaptation:* Modification to the delivery of instruction or materials used rather than modification in content, as that can affect the fulfillment of curriculum goals (Lenz & Schumaker, 1999).

The decisions regarding adaptations must be individualized for each student. The accommodations that are used in assessments must parallel those that are used in instruction and must be based on student strengths. The accommodations and assessments must provide an equal opportunity for students to demonstrate their knowledge. And, lastly, accommodations must be evaluated often and only those that are effective should be continued.

When considering adaptations and accommodations, the over-arching principle is to move students, over time, from dependence to independence. With that in mind, an accommodation that is appropriate at a given point in time may be replaced at a later time with another accommodation that helps the student to be more independent.

Although parents and students must have input into the process, the professionals must make the final decisions as to what is appropriate. There must be ongoing communication between parents and all staff who are implementing these plans (Weinfeld et al., 2006).

Students who are determined to have learning disabilities may qualify for an Individualized Educational Program (IEP) or a 504 Plan (see pp. 146–147). However, students with ADHD may not qualify for either. Nevertheless, teachers and other professionals who recognize attentional issues in their students can effectively use interventions in the classroom to help address the problems that impact student learning.

Best Practice 5: Learn, Teach, Practice, and Model Strategies That Support and Empower Students Who Have Difficulties Related to ADHD

Ms. R. reads the prominent research and literature suggested by her counselor and school psychologist, attends school in-service workshops, speaks with her professional colleagues, talks to her students' doctors, and uses the resources and materials available regarding children with learning difficulties. She individualizes instruction and chooses the appropriate strategies for her children. She learns, teaches, practices, and models the best practices.

It is of the utmost importance that teachers keep abreast of the advancements in current research related to this student population so that the activities and materials used in the classroom are most effective. The following list of categories and strategies can be helpful as a structure for the educator's storehouse of information (Dendy, 2006; DuPaul & Eckert, 1998; McIntyre, 2004; U.S. Department of Education, 2004):

- Classroom Environment

  - Mutually respectful
  - Accepting
  - Exciting
  - Flexible
  - Organized materials
  - Additional classroom supplies available
  - Student placement away from distractions
  - Permission for student to move freely
  - Student choices
  - Positive reinforcement

- Classroom Management

  - Post rules in room
  - Post routines and schedules in room
  - Teacher gives verbal and visual cues and prompts
  - Clear directions are repeated and directions are simplified

- Academics

  - Strength-based instruction
  - Differentiation
  - Modify pace
  - Alternative products
  - Ongoing evaluation
  - Peer tutoring

- Adaptations/Accommodations (IEP/504 Plan)

  - Extended time
  - Task modification

- ◆ Break tasks into segments
- ◆ Frequent breaks
- ◆ Strategy training
- ◆ Interim deadlines
- ◆ Highlight key points, words, directions
- ◆ Preferential seating
- ◆ Student assignment sheet/pad/notebook
- ◆ Allow "fidget toys"
- ◆ Additional textbooks for home

- Technology

  - ◆ Computers
  - ◆ Spell checkers
  - ◆ Calculators

- Social/Emotional

  - ◆ Positive reinforcement
  - ◆ Promote student awareness
  - ◆ Use contracts
  - ◆ Teach social skills

- Behavior Management

  - ◆ Develop good rapport with student
  - ◆ Implement a plan or develop an functional behavioral analysis and behavioral intervention plan with the school team
  - ◆ Reinforce positive behavior
  - ◆ Selectively ignore inappropriate behavior
  - ◆ Develop a token or reward system
  - ◆ Assign responsibilities that require self-control

In addition, many resources for teachers detail appropriate adaptations and accommodations that address students' disabilities, allowing them to understand and present mastery of the material in a manner appropriate to their strengths. An eclectic collection of "what works" is necessary for a teacher to have in order to meet the specific needs of students with ADHD. Once the teacher has acquired information, the teacher can then plan and model the best practices.

Best Practice 6: Teach Students Self-Advocacy Skills

Self-advocacy is when students let others know about who they are and what they need. Ms. R. meets with Sammy to discuss what it means to be a self-advocate. They discuss the following: Who I am! (Strengths and Needs); What I Need! (Adaptations and Accommodations); Which Tools Work For Me? (Interventions and Strategies); and How to Get What I Need to Succeed! (Weinfeld et al., 2006; see Appendix A). When Sammy is able to articulate his own strengths and needs, he will learn to write a self-advocacy letter and will practice his self-advocacy plan verbally. He will be able to communicate this plan to any adult in and out of the school setting in order to receive appropriate support.

Students need to be empowered, not enabled, as they become involved in their learning. Once they are provided with tools, strategies, and skills for learning, students can successfully develop and use their intellect. Students have responsibilities as learners. In order to be successful, they must recognize and accept both their strengths and needs, and gain an understanding of how they learn (metacognition). Once they are aware of their specific issues, students can become active in learning and practicing strategies for thinking, organization, communication, problem solving, and the use of technology. They are expected to complete assignments, become self-directed, and seek help and support as needed. Learning and practicing strategies for developing self-efficacy (the belief in self) and self-advocacy (the ability to tell others what one needs) make it possible for these students to become risk-takers and lifelong learners. Over time, students develop the skills and maturity that allow them to become partners in making decisions regarding their Individualized Educational Programs (Weinfeld et al., 2006). For students with ADHD, self-control and self-management may be particularly challenging and, for this reason, the emphasis on taking responsibility for their learning, where possible, is doubly effective.

The social-emotional needs of these students are as important as the educational ones. With few exceptions, social-emotional issues contribute to the lack of achievement. It is important to see whether negative behaviors and attitudes are the result of an inadequate program or personal issues. For some students, placement in an appropriate program that attends to their gifts and offers support for their learning needs will result in a positive turnaround in behavior and attitude. The development of skills and competencies in the social-emotional realm contribute and complement the other best practices that promote success. Social-emotional health matters inside the classroom and beyond. Students need tools and practice to develop self-efficacy, or the ability to know and to believe in one's self. They need to learn how to say, "I can do this." They need tools and practice for becoming self-advocates, or the ability to know one's self and represent one's self with others. For example, they have to learn to tell an instructor about their needs (e.g., "I am really listening, but I have trouble sitting still. May I get up and quietly walk to the back of the room and then return to my seat?").

The goal is that students see themselves as successful learners by knowing who they are, what they need, which tools work for them, and how to get what they need to succeed. Self-confidence is a critical asset in school success for students with ADHD.

Best Practice 7: Communicate Openly With Parents and Others

Sammy's parents and Ms. R. communicate regularly throughout the school year. The daily assignment sheet is ongoing, as is a weekly progress report. They set up an e-mail correspondence when it is needed and parent/teacher conferences are held periodically to address Sammy's progress. Permission is received for Ms. R. to be in contact, when necessary, with Sammy's doctors.

The general educator keeps the lines of communication open between students, staff, and parents/guardians. When all parties work respectfully to establish open and direct communication, a lasting partnership is possible. Parents should not hesitate to contact their child's teacher with concerns and also should be willing to provide praise when they recognize that a teacher is working effectively with their child. The same goes for teachers: Parents need to know about both the problems, concerns, and worries regarding their child *and* the good things teachers see the child doing. Discussing the child's strengths or progress with parents in a positive manner can build student self-confidence, leading to more academic success.

Middle School and High School

When Sammy completed his elementary school years and entered middle and high school, his attentional issues still needed to be addressed. However, the strategies he learned and his growing ability to be a self-advocate made his transition to secondary education less problematic. Sammy had internalized those strategies that worked for him. These included:

- preferential seating,
- task analysis of assignments,
- daily assignment notebook,
- use of highlighters for key words and concepts,
- social skills training learned with counselor,
- use of assistive technology, and.
- self-advocacy.

Sammy, attending his own IEP meeting with his parents and school staff, created a plan to be utilized in his new school setting. The plan included continuing strategies that Sammy found successful and other strategies, such as:

- working with his teachers on cues for attention,
- permission to move freely in the classroom when necessary,
- choice for alternative products and hands-on activities,
- unobtrusive assignment notebook check,
- periodic student/teacher conferencing, and
- interim checks on long-term assignments.

Sammy's parents created an action plan with Sammy and the staff. Recognizing that Sammy was responsible for his learning and also recognizing the importance of the possible negative effects of providing excessive or unnecessary accommodations, the need to select accommodations based on the impact of the individual student's disability, the need to move students from dependence to independence, and the need to evaluate and revise adaptations and accommodations, Sammy and the school team chose the relevant interventions and built in a periodic evaluation on his progress. Appropriate changes would occur to make sure that Sammy was a successful learner (Weinfeld et al., 2006). Sammy had already learned skills in landscape design from his architect mentor. He was a regular helper in leading students to beautify his elementary school and led a part-time work team mowing lawns in his neighborhood and improving landscaping with the help of a landscape designer identified by his mentor.

As Sammy's story shows, accommodations and educational interventions for students with ADHD do not end when they leave the elementary school setting. Because of the differences in the way middle and high schools do scheduling and the addition of electives, students will need to learn to be strong self-advocates, vocalizing their needs and preparing to adapt to new accommodations as their needs change with the change in environment.

Middle school and high school may be difficult for any student. For many kids with ADHD, the secondary experience may be more than difficult; it may be totally overwhelming. Students with ADHD often face the following challenges:

- academic intensity;
- hormonal changes;
- social issues;
- peer relationships;
- peer teasing, bullying, and rejection;
- establishing relationships with the opposite sex;
- experimenting with illegal substances; and
- driving safely.

According to middle and high school teachers across the country, the adolescent with ADHD also may be faced with the following issues (Dendy, 2000, 2006; Dendy & Zeigler, 2003):

- completing and submitting homework on time,
- forgetting homework assignments,
- disorganization,
- motivation and persistence,
- specific academic challenges,
- issues with planning ahead,
- disruptive behavior,
- issues with following directions,
- difficulty understanding expectations, and
- executive functioning deficits.

The best practices and effective teaching strategies used in the elementary years are transferable and applicable to the teenage years. It is essential to build and protect self-esteem through having a skill-based school identity. Based on updated evaluations and data, the appropriate adaptations, modifications, and accommodations must be implemented. The individualized academic and behavioral interventions will help the student with ADHD succeed in secondary school. Once again, all of the stakeholders must engage in ongoing communication. Most importantly, the student must be responsible for her own learning and take a more active role in the educational process.

It is important to realize that girls with ADHD have unique challenges during the middle and high school years. Girls with ADHD are overlooked because they often are not discipline problems. They often work harder in order to hide their deficiencies. They do, however, struggle with social, emotional, and hormonal issues and stress from society's stereotypical expectations that girls should be sweet, passive, neat, eager to please, and sensitive. Girls have many of the same academic and executive functioning issues as boys.

In addition, as students age, those students with an IEP will need to begin to take larger roles in the IEP process. This may begin with the student sitting in on the meetings and vocalizing what works best for him or her. As the student gets closer to the age of 18, however, he or she must begin leading IEP meetings and develop a strong self-understanding of his or her needs in preparation for postsecondary education, where the individual student is responsible for ensuring that he or she receives the best education. See Chapter 8 on college for more information.

Additional Student Needs

Throughout this book, the authors have stated that the genetic, medical, psychological, environmental, educational, and personal components of each child differ. Therefore, we ask readers to remember that Sammy is just one profile of a child with attentional issues. He is a model success story, where everything has gone right, because of informed and conscious planning. Although the best practices listed work with all children, the specifics will be vastly different from one child to another. For example, Sammy does not exhibit major behavior problems that some students show in the school setting. If Sammy had challenging behaviors, the teacher would include strategies to address them. DuPaul and Stoner (2002) offer excellent guidance for interventions that address academic behavior problems, including using more than one intervention strategy, combining proactive and reactive strategies to prevent and manage problem behaviors, individualizing interventions, and implement strategies close to the time and place that specific behaviors occur.

As teachers study a student's profile and work with other professionals, individualized intervention plans are developed that reflect the appropriate adaptations, modifications, and accommodations needed for that specific child.

Students who are found to have learning disabilities may qualify for an Individualized Educational Plan (IEP). Part of the eligibility determination is based on a decision regarding whether or not the student requires specially designed instruction to meet the unique needs resulting from his or her disability. When it is decided that the student has a disability and needs special instruction, an IEP is developed. The IEP includes goals and objectives and provides a specific plan for direct instruction, as needed. The IEP also includes classroom and testing accommodations (Weinfeld et al., 2006). The categories on an Individualized Education Program (IEP) form provide a structure for data collection and instructional implications. Categories include:

- Student and School Information
- Evaluation Eligibility Data
  - Present Level of Functional Performance
  - Health
  - Physical
  - Behavior
  - Academic achievement
  - Communication
  - Assistive technology

- Service Provider
- Instructional and Testing Accommodations
  - Timing
  - Scheduling
  - Setting

- Supplemental Aids, Services, Program Modification, and Supports
- Postsecondary Goals
- Course of Study
- Transition Services/Activities
- Student Accountability for General Curriculum

All students with attentional issues do not have an IEP. An alternative is the development of a 504 Plan. Like an IEP, a 504 Plan is a result of federal law and can put into place formal accommodations to be used both in the classroom and in testing situations. Unlike an IEP, 504 Plans do not typically provide for special education instruction of any kind. They are administered and monitored by the "general" educators in the school, typically the guidance counselor (Weinfeld et al., 2006). Realistically, some children with attentional issues do not have either an IEP or a 504 Plan, but need adaptations and accommodations. It is therefore imperative that teachers know their students' strengths, needs, and the strategies necessary to support a child in the classroom, whether there is a formal document or not. Less formal contracts or plans should be created in situations where children with ADHD need support in school, but are not eligible for a 504 Plan or IEP.

A child is made up of many parts and all of the parts together make the whole child. By understanding the complexities of the individual, by recognizing that the whole child consists of many facets, and by using a wider lens to see a child, we are better prepared to help the child be successful. School is only one part the child's day. DuPaul and Eckert (1998) concluded that strategies that specifically address academic performance must be part of the treatment for ADHD in order to most beneficially impact educational deficits.

Managing Attention in Special Populations

Attention needs are common in special populations such as children with developmental disabilities, intellectual deficits, autism spectrum disorders, and with neurological impairments such as stroke, traumatic brain injury, and cerebral palsy. Although these attention needs are secondary to the primary disability and are not necessarily diagnosed separately as ADHD, they still respond to the same behavior management approaches.

Gifted Students With ADHD

Bright students who are not reaching their potential present themselves in different ways depending on what is contributing to their lack of achievement. Sometimes their difficulty in school is due to a documented learning disability. Sometimes it may be due to a health impairment such as ADHD.

Diagnosis of ADHD in gifted students can be very difficult. Some of the characteristics used to identify students as having ADHD also are characteristics of gifted students in general, gifted students who have other disabilities (including learning disabilities), and bright underachieving students. It is clear, however that many gifted students, with or without other disabilities, also are impacted by ADHD. Appropriate diagnosis by a mental health professional or doctor is crucial.

In planning it is crucial that the teacher consider instructional methods and strategies that either circumvent the student's difficulties or build in the necessary scaffolding to empower students to be successful with the demands of the assignment (Weinfeld et al., 2006).

Preschool

This chapter has focused on students in elementary school through high school. The majority of children are diagnosed with ADHD after the age of 6 and once they have attended school full-time. It is important, however, to round out the picture with a look at preschoolers.

Some of the common behaviors of concern for preschoolers include attentional issues, disrupting activities, talking excessively, being off task, low frustration levels, and aggressiveness (Dendy, 2006). Diagnosing youngsters who exhibit oppositional behaviors, impulsivity, short attention span, and extreme activity with ADHD is difficult because many of these behaviors are not unusual for many preschoolers. In any preschool or kindergarten class, there may be a very wide variation in early development. Some children are a year or more below or ahead of others in any given skill or readiness to exhibit a skill. Many are still "playing at" being in school when they start school. Social and self-controls vary widely, as well.

A medical exam usually is recommended for youngsters because thyroid problems and other medical conditions often exhibit similar symptoms as ADHD. There is still controversy regarding current legal or best practice guidelines for medicating preschoolers. (Refer to Chapter 3 for coverage about medication issues.)

Citing Lawrence Greenhill, M.D., Schusteff (n.d.) noted that the two behavioral patterns that often predict ADHD diagnosis in later life are preschool expulsion and peer rejection.

Parents of children who were diagnosed with ADHD at age 6 or older often indicate that they knew years before their child was school-aged that there were attentional issues. Teachers who teach preschoolers also are acutely aware of extreme behaviors of children in their classes. It is imperative that parents and teachers communicate with each other regarding the child and work on appropriate interventions on behalf of the child. Tapping the expertise of doctors and institutions like NIMH and CHADD will aid in providing up-to-date information, successful strategies, and effective approaches that address ADHD in very young children.

Whether a child is a preschooler or attends an elementary, secondary, or higher education institution, there are best practices and effective intervention strategies that will help to ensure his or her academic success. In order to ensure school success, educators will want to follow specific strategies that will help students at every level of schooling and at every level of need, including:

- modifying or changing the classroom environment;

- modifying classroom routines, including how and when work is completed;

- improving students' study skills by demonstrating good study habits and environments;

- improving students' organizational skills, including implementing organizers such as planners and daily report cards;

- enhancing peer support of students with disabilities;

- creating an active learning environment that differentiates for different students' strengths and needs;

- improving students' test-taking skills; and

- ensuring completion of homework through communication with parents and clear understandings of the assignments.

It is important that all of the stakeholders—parents, teachers, other professionals, and the students themselves—keep up with current research in order to know about the most effective strategies and techniques available. Web sites and references are included in the Resources section of this book to help locate information about ADHD.

chapter 7

The Power and Techniques of Effective Coaching*

"Coaching isn't a great mystery. It's just hard work, determination, and inspiration at the right moment."

Bob Zuppke, former head football coach, University of Illinois

T H E use of coaching for individuals with ADHD has exploded over the last two decades. Coaching is one part of a multimodal method approach for treating the entire person. An effective multimodal method includes working with psychiatrists, psychologists, school staff, and other professionals trained in the area of ADHD. With the demands of both home and school increasing at a rapid pace, those with this disability need to develop systems in order to survive. From time-management to goal setting, coaching provides an effective framework for persons with ADHD. It is used to help people learn to effectively manage

---

* This chapter was contributed by Jennifer Engel Fisher, M.ED

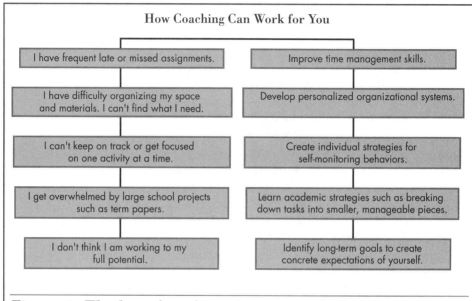

Figure 3. The benefits of coaching for individuals with ADHD.

their school, work, and home life. Figure 3 provides a graphic example of how coaching can work for individuals with ADHD.

It is extremely important to understand what coaching is not. Coaching is not a replacement for therapy. Although both focus on positive interventions and goal setting, a coach usually does not bring the therapeutic skills necessary to treat underlying or comorbid conditions such as anxiety and depression, which commonly coexist with ADHD. Licensed therapists earn an advanced degree in a formal training program. Coaches can be certified by one of the many coaching academies or have an extensive background in working with students with ADHD. Sometimes, therapists and coaches work together in order to treat the "whole person."

An effective coach will work with the student to identify her weaknesses and create an action plan to address her long-term goals by setting short-term goals. A coach does not tell the student what she needs to do; he teaches the student reflective skills in order to promote independence. The power of best practices for coaching is shown throughout the following case study.

Case Study: Identify the Weaknesses and Provide Solutions

Frances, a gifted seventh grader, was diagnosed with ADHD combined type in elementary school. Currently, she was failing all subjects that required writing and was feeling increasingly turned off about school. Although she loved using the computer and was able to collect information on the topics about which she was assigned to write with ease, the first problem Frances encountered was that she was not able to identify what information was important to collect. Therefore, she had too much information, most of it irrelevant.

Although ADHD symptoms differ from person to person, the general approach to coaching uses similar frameworks. For example, while one student waits until the last minute to finish a project, another may be too impulsive and finish it too quickly without checking to see if it contains all the necessary information. The purpose of coaching is for the individual to independently develop internal and external structures (Swartz, Prevatt, & Proctor, 2005). Coaching usually is broken down into four major components (Douglas & Morley, 2000):

- goal-setting,
- assessment,
- awareness and action planning, and
- implementation and monitoring.

The main objective of coaching is to have the student identify his target areas of need and then create an action plan that works toward long-term goals. (Young & Giwerc, 2003) The coach acts as a collaborator, not a counselor or advisor (Quinn, Ratey, & Maitland 2001).

Frances began taking medication to treat her ADHD soon after her diagnosis. At the same time, she had weekly visits to a psychologist who recommended that Frances work with a coach. At first she was reluctant due to her many afterschool activities, and she didn't want to get involved with one more person who claimed to be able to help. After some cajoling, she agreed to meet Jack for one session. She knew her ADHD was impacting her education and she wanted to succeed both in and out of school.

As parents, we want what is best for our children. From choosing the right school to buying the right sneakers, finding the highest quality is always in the front of our minds. Selecting a coach is no exception. Coaching is an umbrella term that encompasses executive coaching, academic coaching, or organizational coaching. Choosing the right coach for your child can be confusing. Finding a coach who builds a trusting and safe relationship with the student is essential and time spent researching coaches is crucial.

Coaches should have training specific to the needs of individuals with ADHD. Some are certified while others use their life experiences as their credentials. The Attention Deficit Disorder Association (ADDA) Subcommittee on ADHD Coaching (2002) created the following list of questions to keep in mind when finding a coach:

- How long has the coach practiced?
- What is his or her experience in the coaching profession?
- By whom and when was he or she trained?
- Is this coach certified?
- Does he or she have a specialty (executive coaching, spiritual coaching, career coaching, etc.)?
- Does he or she associate with other coaches belonging to coaching organizations?
- Does the experience of this coach match my needs?
- What else would I like to know about this coach and his or her work in order to discern that we might work well together? (How will the coach work with my child?)

- How exactly would we work together to accomplish what I need to achieve? (How will the coach work with my child as part of a team?; ¶25)

The logistics of working with a coach are equally important. Although this service is meant to be short term, many individuals may choose to keep in contact with their coaches after their initial 6–8 week consultations via phone calls or e-mail. When selecting a coach the following also should be considered:

- Where will these coaching sessions take place?
- Does the coach offer phone or e-mail services?
- How long will each session be?
- What would an individual session look like?
- How, where, and when would we meet?
- What happens if I miss a session?

Reluctantly, Frances sat down with her coach, Jack, for an initial meeting. Because Frances had so much difficulty with her writing, her coach asked her a series of questions instead of having her fill out a form. Frances explained the how and why she came to meet with a coach, as well as answered the following:

- What are your strengths?
- What are your interests?
- What do you feel you need help with?
- What are some long-term goals you hope to accomplish during coaching?

Once Frances began speaking, she couldn't stop. She was amazed how easily the information flowed out of her and how comfortable she felt with sharing this information with Jack. The coach inquired about Frances' symptoms such as distraction, impulsivity, task-completion, and forgetfulness—all effects of her ADHD.

The initial coaching session should cover the following major points:

1. Explain the process of coaching.

2. Discuss the participant's needs and goals.

3. Establish guidelines.

4. Identify the participant's preferred learning style and personal strengths.

5. Set up the coaching schedule.

6. Create a contract with rules and consequences.

7. Set long-term goals.

8. Set weekly goals.

It may sound like a lot of information to cover in one session, but remember that this intake sets the tone for the coaching relationship. The meetings will become a strategizing session in order to find solutions for the student's areas of difficulty. The coach will provide feedback, as well as modify any goals, timeframes, and motivators in order to keep the client on track.

What Is the Difference Between Long- and Short-Term Goals?

A long-term goal refers to the final outcome desired by the client. Earning a B in an English class or learning how to maintain an organized planner are examples of long-term goals. Some clients may want to learn how to manage their time in order to pay bills, complete their work, and balance a social life. It is important to note that some long-term goals may extend past the 6–8 week coaching contract. Short-term goals are the smaller steps in order to meet the long-term goal.

Heacox (1991) created a list of questions used to identify both long- and short-term goals. These are discussion questions that guide the intake sessions as well as follow-up meetings.

- What is one area of my school or life performance I want to improve?
- What is one thing I can do to accomplish my long-term goal?
- How can this short-term goal be broken down into a step-by-step plan?
- What is good about doing this? What are the benefits to me?
- What are the things that might get in my way as I work toward my goal?
- What special materials or help will I need to reach my goal?
- How will I reward myself when I achieve my goal?
- How will I check on my progress and make sure that my plan is working?
- How will I remind myself of my goal?
- How is my plan working? Is it working well? If not, why not?
- Does my plan need to be revised?
- Is the goal still necessary, important, and appropriate?
- Is the incentive right?
- Have I reached my goal?

After answering some brief and probing questions, Frances identified one long-term goal: Writing an effective and accurate research report. Using self-reflection techniques, Frances and Jack created a calendar to set up her short-term goals (see Figure 4).

Frances couldn't believe how manageable this project would be! Living with ADHD had been so difficult that she could not see the light at the end of the tunnel. Frances and Jack first plugged in the activities, such as softball, that were prior commitments into her calendar. Then, in a different color, the English assignment was broken down into manageable pieces. The coach then suggested that Frances use an electronic planner with an alarm to remind her how much time she was working on each section. It also would help her

Sunday	Monday	Tuesday	Wednesday	Thursday	Friday	Saturday
	Meet with Jack Confirm which questions I will choose for my paper. Create calendar	Create a list of criteria needed to get a "B." Begin outline	Softball practice	2:30 p.m.–4 p.m.: Research topic and collect information based on the outline	10 a.m.–12 p.m.: (With a short break) Finish research	Softball game
12 p.m.–1:30 p.m.: First two paragraph due (45 minutes–no break)	Plans with friends	5 p.m.–7 p.m.: (With a break) Next three paragraphs due	Softball practice	4:30 p.m.–6 p.m.: (With a break) Work on paragraphs	Day off	Softball game
Rough draft of English paper competed	Final look-over of paper Softball practice	**English paper due**				

Figure 4. Calendar sequence for Frances' English paper goals.

remember to take breaks. Frances never realized that taking a break was OK.

Coaching Versus Peer Tutoring

Peer tutoring can be defined as any instructional strategy wherein two students work together on an academic activity with one student providing assistance, instruction, and feedback to the other

(Greenwood, Maheady, & Carta, 1991). It has been shown that peer tutoring increases engagement in an activity as well as academic performance (DuPaul & Eckert, 1998). Although a number of peer tutoring models exist, Pfiffner and Barkley (1990) identified similar instructional characteristics:

1. working one-to-one with another individual,

2. instructional pace determined by learner,

3. continuous prompting of academic responses, and

4. frequent and immediate feedback about the quality of the performance.

There are several key points to keep in mind when deciding to work with a peer tutor that are similar to those when considering working with a coach. The first step would be to inquire about the training the peer tutor has and if it matches your child's areas of need. Remember the reason a coach or peer tutor is hired. Ask yourself the following: "What is my child going to gain from this experience?" "What are the objectives for my child?"

Classwide Peer Tutoring (CWPT; Greenwood, Delquadri, & Carta, 1988) is one of the most commonly used systems. For about 20 minutes, the class is divided into two teams then they form tutoring pairs within each team. Next, students take turns tutoring each other and the teacher provides the tutors with academic scripts. The tutors provide praise and points for correct answers. Incorrect answers have an immediate opportunity for practice. The teacher monitors the tutoring pairs and awards bonus points for those who are following the directions. Points are earned by each student and tallied at the end of the class. The implications of CWPT on students with ADHD showed an increase in active engagement, as well as test performance in elementary school students.

Coaching is an effective method for students of all ages in order to identify their strengths, needs, and goals. Setting long- and short-term goals, one can improve time-management, organizational, and academic successes, as well as other executive functioning skills. Although a long-term goal can take several weeks, months, or even a full school semester or year to achieve, there is an end in sight. Selecting the right coach, establishing a supportive and trusting relationship, and "keeping your eye on the prize" is a win-win experience for all.

chapter 8

College and Beyond

"Our greatest glory is not in never falling, but in rising every time we fall."

Confucius

A S parents, involvement with a child's education does not end on the last day of high school. Continuing to offer support and guidance and, at the same time, expecting the adolescent to apply his or her emerging self-advocacy and responsible behavior to a postsecondary setting is important.

It is imperative for the student with ADHD who has relied on the modifications and accommodations in the past to act proactively; this includes choosing the right college, technical school, or profession. In August of 2008, The Higher Education Opportunity Act (HEOA) was passed, which included the establishment of a coordinating center to develop inclusive comprehensive transition and postsecondary programs for students with disabilities. This new authorization will allow students with disabilities such as ADHD an easier transition to the post high school years.

Although transition planning starts at age 14 at IEP meetings based on IDEA laws, it continues to be an area of need in American education. The interface between a child's strengths and the realties of the ever-changing requirements of the world of work rarely coordinate as effectively as they should. Many young people are finding themselves changing majors in college. About 25% of college students transfer colleges after the first year. Also, many students who may have once had the protection of 504 Plans and IEPs find themselves without the proper documentation to restart the protections they received through special education eligibility during their early school years.

Choosing a College

For the adolescent or adult with ADHD, choosing a college or university can be a difficult task. It is important to recognize that there are differences in the supports that are available at various institutions. However, by law, all colleges and universities that receive any federal funding must provide "reasonable accommodations" for students with ADHD (CHADD, 2003a, ¶4).

At some colleges and universities, there is very little staff available to provide support services to students with ADHD. These colleges and universities only provide the minimum services required by the law. However, other postsecondary institutions provide extensive support services through specific Student Disability Services/Support Offices and staff members, as well as encouragement to students with ADHD. Finding such a school with appropriate support services and a positive approach toward students with ADHD usually takes some careful research. CHADD (2003a) recommends contacting the Student Disability Service/Support Office of prospective colleges to discuss the following questions:

- Is the head of student disability services a specialist in ADHD and LD issues?

- If not, is there an ADHD–LD specialist on the staff of student disability services?

- How long has the individual in charge of ADHD–LD support been employed at your school?

- Has there been an organized program to educate faculty members about supporting students with ADHD and LD?

- How many students with ADHD are registered with your office?

- Is there a study skills program at your school specifically designed for students with ADHD problems such as organization, time management, and planning?

- Is there an ADHD student support group on campus?

- Do members of your staff actively advocate for students with ADHD when they encounter resistance to accommodations from a faculty member?

- Does a member of your staff participate in freshman orientation, helping students with ADHD and their families better understand and access services from your office?

- Does your office provide specialized registration assistance to students with ADHD?

- Do students with ADHD automatically receive priority registration privileges at your school?

- Is there a physician affiliated with student health services who can prescribe stimulant medication for students with ADHD?

- Do you maintain a list of appropriate, experienced professionals in the community who can provide extra support such as counseling, psychotherapy, or ADHD coaching?

- In general, would you describe your institution as having a welcoming and supportive attitude toward students with ADHD? (¶5)

Although very few schools will answer all of these questions in a way that seems to make it the perfect match for the college student with ADHD, it is important to look for a school that provides answers that seem supportive to students with ADHD. These answers indicate better chances that a student with ADHD will succeed at that school. CHADD (2003a) states that it is a good idea for postsecondary students with ADHD to look for schools with the following:

- a focus on quality teaching,

- small class sizes,

- opportunities for classroom participation, and

- faculty members who take an individual interest in students.

Students with ADHD looking for postsecondary educations have many resources for locating good programs that address their learning needs. Many books can be found at local libraries and bookstores. There also are specialists who consult with families of children with special needs on finding the right college "fit." However, such specialists can be costly. Often, students and parents willing to put in enough time and effort to visit colleges and ask questions about the schools' disability services can find good fits for postsecondary education.

College Issues for Students With ADHD

ADHD often continues to impact students at the college level. These difficulties, which also often impact students at other levels of education, include issues that are related to both schoolwork and personal issues.

Achievement struggles often include:

- poor organization,

- poor time management,

- difficulty concentrating and focusing (often impeding reading),
- poor note-taking and writing skills,
- difficulty completing assignments,
- problems completing homework,
- difficulty preparing for tests, and
- struggles in learning how to study.

Personal struggles frequently include:

- feelings of frustration,
- poor self–esteem,
- inappropriate social skills,
- too much time socializing,
- problems in relationships,
- confusion about goals and the future,
- lack of perseverance or procrastination, and
- lack of sleep and difficulty getting up in the morning.

Frequently, college students with ADHD incorrectly assume that following graduation from high school, they do not need supports or treatment for their ADHD. They also may take too many courses in college and, due to their unrealistic expectations, not take into account other demands on their time. Often, college students with ADHD struggle with time management and stay up all night either studying or partying and end up sleeping throughout the following day.

Getting accommodations in college can help address some of these issues. Accommodations can include, but are not limited to:

- note-taking services,
- extended time on tests,

- copies of professor's notes,
- use of the writing center,
- tutoring,
- preferential seating, and
- regularly scheduled appointments with a counselor.

College students with ADHD can implement other techniques to increase their chances for success. It is important for these students to develop effective strategies for self-care, including getting enough rest and exercise and learning and implementing strategies to reduce their levels of stress and manage their time effectively. Establishing supportive relationships in college, either with peers in a study group or a coach, also can be quite beneficial. Frequently, a team of professionals is most effective in helping the college student with ADHD to set appropriate goals and priorities and effectively carry them out. Such a team often includes a physician, a counselor, and/or a coach. As a result, the goal is for the student to adopt an educated decision-making process, whereby the student takes responsibility for his or her own behaviors and learns to prioritize on his or her own.

In some cases, students with ADHD may yet lack the requisite maturity for college. They may seek to transfer for the wrong reasons. Sometimes a year off in the world of work or volunteer service may help the student mature and reflect on goals.

Obtaining Assistance in College

In order to apply for services from the disabilities office as a student with ADHD, a recent ADHD assessment for college accommodations often is required. Such an evaluation typically requires an assessment of intellectual functioning, learning style, and academic strengths and weaknesses.

The process of applying for services and the procedure for reviewing a student's eligibility for services differs among the various colleges and universities. Students who have been diagnosed with ADHD are able to choose whether or not to disclose their condition during the admissions process. Sometimes the general application includes an opportunity, but not a requirement, to disclose and apply for disability services. If, however, applying for the disabilities services program is a separate process, which it frequently is, the student will benefit from completing the application at the same time as he applies for admission to the college or shortly after he is accepted for admission to the college. Often, students decide to provide documentation in the general application because this information can help the college understand their strengths, while taking into account any weaknesses that can be explained by the ADHD diagnosis. The submission of documents does not guarantee that a student with ADHD is eligible for special services in college.

In submitting documentation for a disability, the following documents are commonly required:

- a letter from a professional describing the disability and discussing the current academic impact,

- a recent psychological evaluation that diagnoses the disability and states the date of the diagnosis, and

- a current IEP or 504 Plan from high school that documents the provided accommodations and services.

Some colleges only require a prior IEP or 504 Plan from high school. As a general rule, an IEP, 504 Plan, or evaluation should not be more than 3 years old.

Case Study: The College Experience

The following case study provides a good example of how students with ADHD can benefit from working one-on-one with a professional who understands their disability and the college setting. In this case, the student uses a coach (see Chapter 7) to assist her in her learning needs. However, at many universities, students are assigned to a particular staff member in the Disability Services/Support Office who can implement many of the same strategies.

Melissa was struggling in college across every subject area. Now that she was attending college, her IEP was no longer in effect. She now has a 504 Plan, which allows her extended test time, preferential seating, and other modifications and accommodations. She shared the plan with her teachers, but still had difficulties in college. Melissa easily accepted her recent diagnosis of ADHD and was eager to work with a coach to guide her through this process.

By the time she began working with an ADHD coach, she had already repeated English 101 and had difficulties in her Criminology class. In order to receive a grade in her English and Criminology classes, she would have to complete the missing assignments over the summer. That is when she met Stacey. Stacey was not only an ADHD coach, but also had her master's degree in Special Education, which appealed to Melissa.

After filling out a questionnaire as well as speaking with her coach, she determined that she needed help in the following areas:

- finding a better approach to schoolwork,
- not feeling overwhelmed,
- completing multiple assignments,
- keeping track of her assignments,
- breaking down tasks into manageable pieces,
- goal setting for those smaller tasks, and
- efficiency.

The coach, sensing Melissa's anxiety with completing multiple assignments over the summer, realized some academic coaching also would be appropriate. They began breaking down her first English assignment. This was exceptionally difficult because the assignment called for choosing a question to respond to and Melissa had a difficult time making choices.

Working together, they designed the following:

1. Read all of the questions you can choose from.
2. Narrow the questions down to the three you are most interested in.
3. Create a brief outline for the three questions you narrowed it down to.
4. Chose one question based on the outlines.
5. Break down the question based on punctuation and key words.
6. Create index cards related to the question's key words and topics.
   a. Put each topic/word on its own card.
   b. Manipulate the cards to form an outline/framework
   c. Look at how the cards relate to each other.
   d. Recognize that a thought can be put on more than one card to provide more detail to the outline.
7. Take the organized cards and create a table, filling in information based on her knowledge and examples from the book.
8. Support each opinion with one of the examples from the book.

At their second meeting, Melissa was visibly anxious. She stated that although she completed her English paper, she did not follow the exact calendar and was upset with herself for not staying on target. She felt that her ADHD was unmanageable. Her coach, Stacey, revisited their goals generated from their last meeting and showed Melissa everything she did accomplish. After 5 minutes of discussion, they both realized a new long-term goal: To manage multiple projects with realistic deadlines. The calendar that was created at the first meeting appeared wonderful, but it was not realistic for Melissa.

She felt overwhelmed when she missed a deadline and once that date passed, she felt "Why bother?" A new system needed to be created.

Another "aha" moment came to Melissa at this meeting: It was OK to ask for more frequent check-ins from Stacey. Once she missed her interim deadlines, she felt so upset with herself. When Stacey called or e-mailed her on specific dates to keep her on track, Melissa felt like she was not alone. The purchase of a personal digital assistant (PDA) was the incentive/reward for completing her next project.

Melissa also began contacting her school's support office to see what other resources were available.

ADHD in Adulthood

According to the American Academy of Child & Adolescent Psychiatry (AACAP, 2008; see http://www.aacap.org for more information), ADHD begins in childhood, but it often lasts into adolescence and adulthood. AACAP notes that several studies done in recent years estimate that between 30% and 65% of children with ADHD continue to have symptoms into adolescence and adulthood. It has been estimated that approximately eight million adults in the United States suffer from ADHD, making it the second most common psychological problem in adults after depression ("New Research," n.d.).

Recognizing and diagnosing ADHD in adulthood sometimes can be difficult. According to NIMH (2008a), when a child is diagnosed with ADHD, frequently a parent will concurrently recognize that he or she has a number of similar symptoms. A child's diagnosis and, therefore, a parent's recognition of his or her own symptoms may, for the first time, provide an understanding of some of the traits that have given the parent trouble for years. In adulthood, these traits may include distractibility, impulsivity, and restlessness. Other adults may seek professional help for another disorder such as depression or anxiety, but later find out that the initial cause of many of their emotional problems is their ADHD.

Interestingly, a correct diagnosis of ADHD sometimes brings a sense of relief. Adults with attention deficits often have many negative self-perceptions that may have lowered their self-esteem. Therefore, the correct diagnosis of ADHD can begin to help these adults understand their problems and they can then begin to face them. Treatment for ADHD in adulthood often is accompanied by psychotherapy that can help adults recognize and manage the anger they feel about the failure to diagnose the disorder when they were younger and the struggles they have had as a result. Although medication often is helpful and can give needed support, adults with ADHD also will benefit from learning to succeed on their own. Thus, psychoeducation and individual psychotherapy can be helpful. Additionally, a professional coach can help adults with ADHD learn how to better organize their lives. Above all, adults with ADHD benefit from learning as much as they can about their own disorder in order to be able to better advocate for themselves and both seek and utilize resources in their community and from professionals.

As adults, individuals with ADHD often are undereducated relative to their intellectual ability and their family educational background. They also frequently have difficulties with adjusting to work, and may be underemployed in their occupations relative to their own intelligence, education, and family background. Adults with ADHD tend to change jobs more often than other adults. Sometimes job changes are made by these individuals due to boredom or because of interpersonal problems in the workplace. They also tend to have inconsistent friendships and dating relationships and more frequently have marital discord and even divorce. Speeding while driving, receiving traffic citations for this behavior, motor vehicle accidents, and driver's license suspensions or removal are relatively commonplace among adults with ADHD.

As noted in several of the chapters in this book, individuals with ADHD experience a greater likelihood for developing other conditions over the course of their lives, called *comorbidities*. It is important to emphasize here that comorbidities are not just limited to children with ADHD and can affect adults, as well, including young adults

Table 2
Percentages of Individuals With ADHD Who Develop the Following Conditions

Condition	Percentage
Oppositional and defiant behavior	50%
Conduct problems and antisocial difficulties	25%–40%
Learning disabilities	25%–40%
Low self-esteem and depression	25%
Serious mental condition (including bipolar disorder)	5%–10%
Antisocial personality disorder	10%–20%
Legal or illegal substance overuse, dependence, or abuse	10%–25%

attending postsecondary institutions. Table 2 shows the approximate percentage of individuals with ADHD who will develop other conditions during their lives.

Despite the higher risk among individuals with ADHD for developing other conditions, it should be noted that many individuals with attention deficits do not develop these associated conditions.

Challenges in the Work Environment

Adolescents and adults with ADHD may face particular challenges in the work environment, just as children with ADHD face difficulties in school. These challenges can occur in several key areas that are common to most work situations. The following guidelines provided by CHADD (2003b) through the National Resource Center on ADHD (http://www.help4adhd.org), have helped many adolescents and adults with ADHD to improve on-the-job functioning and have helped some individuals with ADHD to have very successful careers (several of these tips also are helpful for children with ADHD to implement in classrooms or study areas):

When individuals with ADHD suffer from *distractibility* in work environments, the following strategies may help:

- Request a private office or quiet cubicle.

- Take work home or work when others are not in the office. This may require requesting "odd" work hours, such as coming in earlier or staying later than your coworkers.

- Use "white noise" earphones, soothing music, or other sounds to drown out office noises.

- Work in unused space, such as a conference room, where there are few distractions.

- Route phone calls directly to voicemail and respond to them at a set time every day. You can also set aside a particular time each hour to respond to e-mails.

- Jot down ideas in a notebook to avoid interruption of the current task.

- Keep a list of ideas during meetings so that you can communicate more effectively. Prepare agendas before meetings if you are leading them to keep you on track.

- Perform one task at a time and do not start a new task until the current one is done.

Adults with ADHD who may struggle with *impulsivity and temper outbursts* in the workplace will likely benefit from trying the following strategies:

- Learn to use self-talk to monitor impulsive actions.

- Work with a coach to role-play appropriate responses to frustrating situations.

- Ask for regular, constructive feedback to become aware of your impulsivity.

- Practice relaxation and meditation techniques. Some workplaces even offer yoga or other lunchtime stress relievers.

- Anticipate the problems that regularly trigger impulsive reactions.

- Develop routines for coping with these triggering situations.

Adults with *hyperactivity* often do better in jobs that allow a great deal of movement, such as sales, but if you have a sedentary job, the following strategies may help:

• Take intermittent breaks to photocopy, go to the mailroom, or walk to the water fountain.

• Take notes in meetings to prevent restlessness.

• Move around, exercise, take a walk, or run up and down the stairs.

• Bring lunch instead of going out to buy it so the lunch hour can be a time for exercise.

To improve *poor memory*, try the suggestions below:

• Use tape recording devices or take thorough notes at meetings. Review notes with colleagues before future meetings to ensure you understand them and remember the context.

• Write checklists for complicated tasks.

• Use a bulletin board, computer program, or other technique for reminders.

• Learn how to use a day planner and keep it with you to keep track of tasks and events.

• Write notes on sticky pads and put them in a highly visible place.

Because of their strong need for stimulation, some adults with ADHD become *easily bored* at work, especially with detailed paperwork and routine tasks. To prevent boredom, try the following tips:

• Set a timer to stay on task.

• Break up long tasks into shorter ones.

• Take breaks, drink water, and get up to walk around.

• Find a job with stimulating responsibilities and minimal routine tasks.

Poor time management can be an issue for adults with ADHD. Here are some guidelines for improving time management skills:

- Use timeline charts to break large projects into smaller pieces, with shorter due date dates for each piece.

- Reward yourself for achieving short-term due dates.

- Use watch or timer devices with alarms or buzzers (some computers do this). Program your computer to beep 5 minutes before every meeting on the calendar.

- Use planners or computer planning software.

- Avoid overscheduling by overestimating how long each task or meeting will take.

Procrastination not only prevents completion of tasks, but also creates problems for others on the team. Here are some strategies for success:

- Break the task into small pieces, rewarding yourself along the way.

- Hire a coach (see Chapter 7) to learn to become accountable for achieving each piece of the task.

- Ask your supervisor to set a deadline for tasks.

- Consider working on a team with a coworker who manages time well. Set up standards for him or her to politely bring you back on task.

Lack of organization of complex or long-term projects is common for adults with ADHD. Managing projects requires a range of skills including time management, organizing materials, tracking progress, and communicating accomplishments. Try the following guidelines:

- Break projects up into manageable parts with rewards for completing each. Set a timeline for completing the smaller pieces of the larger task.

- Ask a coach to assist you in tolerating longer and longer projects, a bit at a time.

- Find and partner with a coworker who has good organizational skills.

- Look for work that requires only short-term tasks.

Lacking organization of materials can lead to delays in turning in reports and timesheets. Poor maintenance of a filing system can create the impression of carelessness. If paperwork is a significant part of the job, try these tips:

- Make it a rule to handle each piece of paper only once or to file it immediately open receipt. Follow your rules.

- Ask an administrative assistant to handle detailed paperwork.

- Keep only those papers that are currently in use and purge the rest.

- Make filing more fun by color-coding folders and using catchy labels.

Poor interpersonal or social skills among adults with ADHD may unintentionally offend coworkers. Often adults with ADHD interrupt others frequently, talk too much, are too blunt, or do not listen. If social skills are a challenge, try the following strategies:

- Ask for feedback, especially if you have had problems with colleagues and supervisors.

- Learn to pick up on social cues more readily.

- Work with a coach (see Chapter 7) to determine what settings often lead to interpersonal/social issues.

- Request to work with coworkers with whom you get along well or who understand your social skills needs.

- Seek a position with greater autonomy if working with others is challenging for you.

The skills and strategies learned over time can be effectively and efficiently transferred and applied to a variety of life experiences. Recognizing personal strengths and needs, utilizing appropriate resources, and proactively accessing guidance and support necessary can ultimately lead to success in college and the work place.

chapter 9

The Part Technology Plays in Managing ADHD

"We're changing the world with technology."

Bill Gates

THROUGHOUT the last several decades, rapid growth in the area of technology has impacted our lives. Similarly, over the years there has been a significant increase in the types of technological options available for assisting individuals with ADHD. Technology is important because it can open new opportunities for accessing education and can help break down the barriers to learning for children and adolescents with ADHD. Some of this technology is available through mental health professionals, while other technology can be used directly in the school and home environments.

Although this chapter will explore the current technology available to assist in the school success of children with attention deficits, technology changes exponentially over time. Therefore, it is imperative that professionals, parents, and other people involved in the lives of individuals with ADHD keep abreast of the new technology and how it can be used to support people with ADHD.

Neurofeedback

Neurofeedback, otherwise known as electroencephalogram (EEG) biofeedback, has been used to treat ADHD since the 1970s (Lubar, Swartwood, Swartwood, & O'Donnell, 1995). Although neurofeedback originally was deemed as poorly researched and not worth the excitement it generated when it first came out, neurofeedback has gained empirical support over time. Therefore, it is now practiced more widely in treating individuals with ADHD and has recently gained greater acceptance from mental health practitioners working with individuals with attention issues.

Neurofeeback is based on the theory that most individuals with ADHD have increased slow-wave brain activity and decreased fast-wave brain activity in comparison to their peers. The goal of neurofeedback is to guide people to learn to independently regulate their own brain activity. This process is taught by using a video game that provides immediate feedback to the individual with ADHD about his or her brainwave activity. Using electrodes attached to the top of an individual's head, the brain's electrical activity is measured and then processed by an electroencephalograph (EEG) and displayed on the computer. Before starting the game, the client is trained about brainwaves and shown the goal—the types of brainwaves he or she is supposed to produce. Each time the client's brainwaves meet the goal he or she is immediately rewarded with positive feedback in the video game. As the individual gains more practice utilizing the feedback, he or she reduces the amount of slow-wave brain activity and/or increases the amount of fast-wave brain activity. Individuals with ADHD have been shown to decrease their symptoms of inattention and hyperactivity after completing a course of neurofeedback training sessions. Some research has shown that neurofeedback outcomes are similar to the outcomes of taking stimulant medication (Rossiter, 2004).

According to Butnik (2005), neurofeedback is an effective intervention for individuals with ADHD that provides an alternative to medication. He states that neurofeedback is particularly helpful for individuals with ADHD who are unable to take traditional medications due to health complications, as well as for individuals with ADHD who have experienced negative reactions to medication. He continues that neurofeedback is safe and typically has no side effects.

According to Loo and Barkley (2005), although there are several existing studies of EEG biofeedback that assert promising results for treating ADHD, the effectiveness of EEG biofeedback to treat ADHD cannot be determined without further studies that examine the effectiveness of the treatment more thoroughly. Although Loo and Barkley comment that it would be helpful to develop nonmedical treatments for ADHD that are efficacious as well cost effective, they state that there is a need to do more research to show that EEG biofeedback provides this effective alternative to medication. These researchers express concern that the EEG biofeedback itself may not be the cause of the reduction in ADHD symptoms. Instead, they suggest that it is possible that the decrease in symptoms may just be occurring as a result of more time spent with a mental health professional.

Computerized Cognitive Training—BrainTrain

According to the BrainTrain Web site (Sanford, 2008), cognitive training or brain training is a new technique that shows great promise in the multimodal treatment of ADHD. This system consists of a variety of exercises that are intended to help improve the individual's functioning in several areas that are frequently difficulties for children with ADHD. These domains include sustaining attention, thinking before acting, visual and auditory processing, listening, and reading. According to the BrainTrain Web site, the goal of cognitive brain training is to develop the core abilities and self-control that are necessary precursors for academic success. It indicates that for some individuals it may be beneficial to combine cognitive training and neurofeedback. Additionally, the Web site suggests that this method can be utilized simultaneously with the traditional approaches of psychotherapy, behavior modification, school modifications, family therapy, and parent education to create a successful integrated model.

Working Memory Training—Cogmed

According to their Web site (http://www.cogmed.com; n.d.), Cogmed Working Memory Training is a program developed for children and adults intended to enhance an individual's capacity for using working memory in an effective, efficient, and exciting manner. Cogmed is a company that was founded by Torkel Klingberg, a Swedish brain researcher. The Web site describes Cogmed as a system that allows children and adults to train at home 5 days a week for 5 weeks with a personal coach from a Cogmed Qualified Practice. This coach leads the training using active and engaging exercises and then analyzes the results. The coach also provides encouragement to the individual through weekly phone calls. The company claims that children experience significant improvements in working memory, have decreased problems in attention and impulsivity, and perform better academically after using the Cogmed program.

Attention Training System— Play Attention

Play Attention's Web site (http://www.playattention.com; 2007) describes the company's product as an effective system that improves attention skills, increases positive task behavior and response control, and reduces behavior problems. The system utilizes a helmet with built-in sensors measuring the brainwaves related to focus and cognitive processing. These brainwaves are translated by the system so individuals are able to control a video game through attention alone. With training and coaching, the individual learns to have and maintain focused awareness and also learns the behaviors that detract from it. The goal is for students to gradually learn to generalize their focused awareness to the school setting in order to perform better on educational objectives including reading and attentive listening in the classroom.

Play Attention is intended for users ages 7 to adult with difficulties paying attention. The company generates detailed reports reflecting the individual's progress. Although the results can be seen in as few as 15 hours, on average it requires 40–60 hours of training to attain permanent results.

Kurzweil Assistive Technology

Kurzweil Educational Systems (http://www.kurzweiledu.com; 2006) develops research-based technologies that are intended to help students in elementary school through college with learning challenges succeed academically. The Kurzweil assistive technology programs target reading, writing, and study solutions. The Web site states that the use of assistive technology such as Kurzweil 3000 is an important accommodation for struggling students and that without this type of accommodation sometimes it is nearly impossible for struggling readers to catch back up academically.

In a study (Hecker, Burns, Katz, Elkind, & Elkind, 2002) of how assistive reading software impacted the reading performance of students with attention disorders, the students used this assistive technology software for the majority of a semester in order to read assignments for an English class. The Kurzweil 3000 program provided students a synchronized visual and auditory presentation of the book and incorporated study skills tools for learning how to highlight and take notes effectively. The results suggested that the assistive software permitted the students to pay better attention during the reading, to reduce their distractibility, to read with decreased stress and fatigue, and to be able to read for a longer duration. The program helped the students with attention disorders to read faster, completing reading assignments in a shorter period of time.

Although it did not have a large impact on comprehension for all students, it helped some students who had comprehension that was very poor. According to Hecker et al. (2002), assistive reading software should be considered as an effective intervention and as an accommodation that will assist students who have attention disorders to help compensate for their disorders. The purpose of the Kurzweil system initially was to help people with significant reading decoding problems by providing immediate text-to-speech context, but the technology also may facilitate better attention to text by doing some of the decoding work that might labor attention systems and working memory.

Inspiration Software

Inspiration Software Inc. (see http://www.inspiration.com) developed Kidspiration for kindergarteners through fifth graders and Inspiration for students in grades 6–12. These tools assist students to learn to plan, research, and complete projects effectively using graphic organizers that help students expand simple topics into more detailed writing.

The version for younger children, Kidspiration, provides students with a simple way to use research-based visual learning principles to build graphic organizers by combining pictures, text, and spoken words in order to represent the student's thoughts and information. Kidspiration intends to develop students' achievement by promoting the following skills:

- categorizing and grouping,

- developing emerging literacy skills,

- building comprehension skills, and

- expressing and organizing thoughts.

Inspiration, the version for middle school and high school students, is similar and also relies on visual learning, Students create their own graphic organizers to represent their own ideas and relationships and then use the integrated outlining function to further organize ideas for their writing. This program helps students improve critical thinking, comprehension, and writing skills across a variety of subjects. Inspiration is intended to improve skills in the areas of:

- analyzing complex topics,

- improving writing proficiency, and

- developing planning skills.

The possible benefit of Inspiration software is to provide a skeleton in order to facilitate executive function through guided planning.

Alternatives to Printed Text

Some students with ADHD also may require or benefit from other mediums than standard printed books, such as books on tape. A federally funded national repository known as the National Instructional Materials Access Center (NIMAC) has digital versions of textbooks and other instructional materials that can be easily converted into accessible formats. Created under IDEA 2004, the NIMAC attains digitally formatted books from textbook publishers, and then allows authorized users within the United States to download the material through an online database. Once the download is complete, these files can be used to produce various specialized formats, including Braille, audio, or digital text for elementary or secondary school students that qualify. Books on tape provide a similar benefit as Kurzweil in lifting the burden of attention on decoding and working memory. In addition,

Recording for the Blind and Dyslexic (http://www.rfbd.org) offers services to parents, students, teachers, and educational professionals.

Technology for Better Time Management and School Functioning

Many individuals with ADHD struggle to manage their time effectively and need assistance to develop a better internal sense of time. Frequently, students with ADHD struggle to determine how long it will take to do something or how long it has been between one activity and the next. They frequently need reminders to complete tasks or timers to help them stay on task until it is time for a break.

There are many forms of technology on the market that can help with time management. One type of reminder strategy that often is used by student with ADHD is an alarm clock or a watch that reminds the student throughout the day of his or her responsibilities both at home and at school. One such watch is the WatchMinder, which can be located at http://www.watchminder.com. This watch was developed by a child psychologist to assist children and adults with ADHD to stay focused and manage time effectively. One benefit of the WatchMinder is that the alarm is actually a vibration, a silent alarm/reminder system. Therefore, students in the classroom can wear it with minimal disruption to the user or those around them. The watch includes two modes. A child's parents can set up a daily routine for the child using the Reminder Mode. This watch allows the users to program 30 different activities at a time. The Training Mode can be used to remind and guide particular activities for various types of behavioral modification. For example, the Training Mode could be used with a student with attention deficits to present the training message "PAY ATTN," in order to silently assist the student in remaining focused in school.

Students with ADHD often benefit from the use of a laptop computer for many purposes. One purpose of the laptop is that a large number of students with ADHD have co-occurring motor difficulties (see Chapter 1 for a more in-depth review). These fine motor issues often make it laborious for students to write papers by hand, not to mention the difficulties that many teachers have with reading the penmanship of students with ADHD. Additionally, the laptop computer can be used in place of an assignment book and students with ADHD often find it easier to type their assignments into the computer and keep track of their schedule and homework with the laptop. Parents also often find that communicating with teachers via e-mail provides a regular method of getting feedback from their child's teachers, as well as communicating concerns or information to the teacher. Additionally, technology that is widely used by people without disorders, such as the computer's spell checker function, can be particularly helpful to people with ADHD.

As we continue to learn more about the physiology of ADHD, researchers are able to continuously develop updated technology to address the symptoms of ADHD. It is essential for parents, teachers, and professionals to keep well informed about the research on technology for helping and treating individuals with ADHD.

chapter 10

A Review of Alternative Treatments Parents Can Consider*

> "Choice of attention—to pay attention to this and ignore that—is to the inner life what choice of action is to the outer. In both cases, a man is responsible for his choice and must accept the consequences, whatever they may be."
> W. H. Auden, poet

W E live in an era in which more individuals are seeking alternatives to the traditional Western medical system, and hence, there is a growing trend toward the use of complementary and alternative (CAM) modalities. By definition, "complementary" modalities are used as an adjunct to conventional treatment, and "alternative" modalities are used in place of conventional treatments. There is a broad range of modalities included in the domain of CAM: acupuncture, chiropractic, diet-based therapies, yoga, herbal medicine, and many more.

---

* This chapter was contributed by Shoshana Silverman Belisle, LMSW.

Based on results from a national health survey, the National Center for Complementary and Alternative Medicine reported that 36% of adults are using some form of CAM, and the number rises to 62% when megavitamin therapy and prayer specifically for health reasons are included in the definition of CAM (Barnes, Powell-Griner, McFann, & Nahin, 2004). One oft-cited study found that visits to alternative medicine practitioners in the United States increased from 427 million in 1990 to 629 million in 1997 and that the U.S. public spent an estimated $36 billion to $47 billion on CAM therapies in 1997 (Eisenberg et al., 1998). Tremendous resources, mostly out-of-pocket, are directed toward these therapies.

The medical community now is recognizing the popularity of many such treatments and, based on growing evidence, has slowly begun to incorporate training in these areas into Western medical education, leading to a new form of medicine called *integrative medicine*. This evolution in medicine blends conventional Western medicine with evidence-based alternative, complementary, and indigenous healing traditions, benefiting from ancient healing wisdom, as well as the proof of science. Consumers are drawn to this trend because it emphasizes a more holistic and prevention-oriented, as opposed to symptom management, approach. Additionally, when conventional medicines result in undesirable side-effects, or the intricacies of the health care system lead to frustrations, consumers will explore alternatives, some based on anecdotal evidence or media and Internet advice. These consumers, in particular, need guidance as to safe and evidence-based options so that they are not led astray by unfounded claims.

Less information is available on the national use of CAM among pediatric populations with ADHD. One study conducted at a pediatric hospital in Boston by Chan, Rappaport, and Kemper (2003) found that 54% of parents reported using CAM to treat their child's attention problems. (Interestingly, only 11% ever discussed these treatments with their pediatricians.) The parents who used CAM rated a "natural therapy" and "having more control over treatments" as significantly more important in their choice of therapy than parents who did not use CAM (Chan et al.). This large percentage is consistent with findings of an Australian study in which 64% of respondents had used or were using alternatives to medication to treat their child's ADHD (Stubberfield, Wray, & Parry, 1999). ADHD populations also appear to use CAM more frequently than general pediatric populations.

Given the large numbers of patients and families seeking other health options, issues of safety and efficacy become increasingly important, especially in situations in which patients do not feel comfortable discussing these treatments with their conventional physicians. This chapter may help guide parents and caregivers in understanding CAM treatment for ADHD, so that they might make more informed decisions. It focuses on the modalities that are either most popular or that are backed by the most research, followed by some of the less studied and emerging options.

Dietary Modification

One of the most popular CAM options among those attempted by parents is dietary modification. It is logical that appropriate nutrition affects brain function and behavior. In fact, in one study (Stubberfield et al., 1999), it was the most commonly used alternative treatment for children with ADHD. However, the popular dietary trends for ADHD remain controversial and research has been inconclusive. Diets include the *Feingold diet*, which seeks to eliminate food additives, the *oligoantigenic diet*, in which very little variety is permitted in order to limit possible sensitivities, and a *sugar-restricted diet*. Parents often gravitate to these options; adjusting diets contributes to their feelings of efficacy because the household diet is under their control (Chan, 2002).

The Feingold Diet

In the 1970s, allergist Dr. Benjamin Feingold (1975) found a rise in hyperactivity and learning disabilities among children that appeared to coincide with the rise in use of artificial salicylates in food additives and colorings. He reported behavioral improvement in 50% of children with ADHD when offending foods were eliminated. Based on numerous reviews and a meta-analysis, scientific evidence for the efficacy of the Feingold diet in children with ADHD is lacking, yet there is preliminary evidence suggesting behavioral effects of artificial colors and preservatives on some children (not necessarily with ADHD) who have identifiable sensitivities (Rojas & Chan, 2005). One meta-analysis of 15 double-blind placebo-controlled studies in patients with ADHD reported that artificial colors significantly increased ADHD symptoms but the significance varied for each of the studies cited (Schab & Trihn, 2004, as cited in Curtis & Patel, 2008).

Oligoantigenic Diet

In the oligoantigenic diet, only a few foods are permitted, with the hopes of eliminating possible sensitivity-provoking culprits. In one study, 49 children were included in a placebo-controlled, double-blind study that investigated the effect of an oligoantigenic diet on hyperactive behavior. Whereas more children taking methylphenidate showed an improvement over those on the diet (44% vs. 24%), results indicated that diet could have a positive effect on behavior (Schmidt et al., 1997).

Sugar-Elimination Diet

Despite the popularity of controlling sugar, recent studies have failed to demonstrate a significant association between sugar and behavior (Chan, 2002). Although it is considered controversial that sucrose in and of itself contributes to ADHD, logic and research studies do support switching from a less nutritious diet that is high in artificial flavors, preservatives and refined sugar to one that includes more nutrient-dense foods (Schauss, 1985, as cited in Sadiq, 2007).

Although evidence does not support that any one diet is guaranteed to improve behavior, parents may wish to experiment with dietary modification, especially if they witness frequent changes in their child's behavior after eating certain foods such as those containing dyes or other additives or common allergens such as wheat and dairy. Many families have been experimenting with gluten-free and dairy-free diets upon hearing anecdotal evidence suggesting an improvement in ADHD-related behavior when these foods are eliminated. However, there is no rigorous research to support this claim at this time. The Center for Science in the Public Interest asserts in its publication on diet and ADHD that we should neither ignore, deny, nor exaggerate the effect of diet on behavior (Jacobsen & Schardt, 1999). The power of diet merits consideration.

Essential Fatty Acid Supplementation

There is increasing interest among researchers and the public in the role of essential fatty acids (EFAs; omega-3 and omega-6) in various health conditions. EFAs are described as "essential" because the body cannot make them; therefore they must be obtained from diet. Dietary sources of omega-3 EFAs include fish, fish oil, flaxseed, and walnuts. Omega-6 EFAs can be found in vegetable oils (corn, sunflower, and soybean) and meats. It is known that essential fatty acids are needed for proper brain functioning and may aid in the transmission of nerve impulses (Brue & Oakland, 2002). Fatty acid deficiencies have been implicated in a number of psychiatric conditions, including bipolar disorder and depression.

Several studies have found that children with attention problems or hyperactivity have depletions of EFAs in their red blood cell membranes and/or plasma compared with controls, and that lowest levels of one type of EFAs (DHA) are associated with more severe symptoms (Freeman et al., 2006). In one study, 96 boys ages 6–12 years with and without ADHD were studied to compare behavior and other problems. The authors found that a greater number of hyperactivity/impulsivity problems were reported for students who had lower EFA concentrations (Stevens & Zentall, 1996).

Although the evidence overall is mixed, several studies of EFA supplementation have shown promising results. Use of omega-3 fatty acid supplements has been helpful to ADHD patients in some but not all studies (Curtis & Patel, 2008). In three controlled trials, combined omega-3 (fish oil) and omega-6 (evening primrose oil) supplements have shown therapeutic benefit for children with behavior and learning difficulties.

Dietary Supplements and Herbal Medicine

Several other readily available dietary supplements are supported by anecdotal and/or clinical evidence for ameliorating ADHD symptoms.

Ginkgo Biloba

Ginkgo biloba is a popular supplement that has been found to be somewhat effective for disorders such as dementia and memory impairment. This effect on brain function suggests that the herb may have a useful effect for children with ADHD, especially those who are primarily inattentive (Brue & Oakland, 2002). One study found positive results on the Connors' scales with 74% of children after taking a combination of ginkgo biloba and Panax quinquefolium, an American ginseng extract, for 4 weeks (Lyon et al., 2001).

Pine Bark Extract

Researchers have found favorable results with Pycnogenol, an extract from the bark of the French maritime pine. Participants who took pycnogenol for 4 weeks showed significant reduction of hyperactivity, improved attention and visual-motor coordination and concentration when compared to controls (Trebaticka et al., 2006).

St. John's Wort

Hypericum perforatum, commonly known as St. John's Wort, is a botanical supplement used for a range of mental health conditions such as depression and anxiety. Although not commonly used for ADHD, it deserves note due to its general popularity. A study (Weber et al., 2008) involving 54 children diagnosed with ADHD found that the children given St. John's Wort for 8 weeks saw no improvement compared to those given a placebo.

Vitamins and Minerals

Research has demonstrated that levels of certain vitamins and minerals, including zinc, magnesium, iron, and B vitamins, often are lower in children with ADHD than in control subjects (Sadiq, 2007). It is, therefore, considered logical that restoring optimal levels of these nutrients may provide benefits in behaviors associated with deficiencies. One randomized controlled study found that children with ADHD who had low iron levels showed improvement on the ADHD rating scale and the Clinical Global Impression-Severity when given an iron supplement for 12 weeks. The authors claimed that the iron therapy was well tolerated and the effectiveness was comparable to stimulants (Konofal et al., 2008). A word of caution however: It should be noted that large doses of iron can prove fatal for children.

Magnesium and Vitamin B-6 supplementation for 2 months also was found to reduce hyperactivity and hypermotivity/aggressiveness and improve school attention in children with ADHD symptoms (Mousain-Bosc et al., 2006). Routine supplementation may not be appropriate for all ADHD populations, but may be appropriate and clinically helpful when deficiencies of certain nutrients have been detected.

Homeopathy

Homeopathy is a therapeutic system that originated 200 years ago with a German physician and pharmacologist named Samuel Hahnemann. He found that substances, either natural or manmade, which caused specific disease states in a healthy individual, could be used to *treat* the same symptoms in someone who is ill. Therefore, the fundamental principle is that of "similars" or of treating "like with like." No one quite understands the mechanisms of action in homeopathy, and it is that much more mysterious because the substances are so diluted that essentially only the "energetic" quality of the substance remains. A very detailed therapeutic system, classic homeopathy does not have uniform medicines that are routinely given for particular diagnoses. Rather, medicines are chosen very carefully for each patient based on a complex symptom and constitutional picture that the homeopath assesses during a thorough health intake interview. It should be noted that homeopathy is taught in medical schools in Europe and Asia and therefore is not considered alternative. Families often will use it as a first-line treatment because homeopathy carries fewer stigmas culturally (Sadiq, 2007).

Several clinical trials have shown promising results for treating ADHD with homeopathy. Lamont (1997) assigned 43 children with ADHD to either placebo or homeopathic treatment in a double blind, partial crossover study. The homeopathic remedy used in the study included *Stramonium*, a treatment for nervousness and terrors; *Cina*, a treatment for restlessness; and *Hyoscyamus niger*, a treatment for poor impulse control. Children were given either the homeopathic remedy or a placebo for 10 days, after which parents or caregivers rated the children on the amount of ADHD-related behaviors they displayed using a 5-point scale. Those receiving the homeopathic remedy displayed significantly fewer behaviors, and benefits persisted for 2 months despite discontinuation of treatment.

A Swiss randomized, placebo controlled, crossover trial that involved 83 children with ADHD (Frei et al., 2007) found a small but significant benefit from treatment according to parent ratings on core symptoms. An interesting finding of this trial was demonstrated during the "open-label" (non-blind) screening phase. During this screening phase, each child's response to successive homeopathic medications was observed until the optimal medication was identified. During the screening phase, 84% of the children responded to treatment and reached eligibility for the randomized portion of the study. This took an average of 5 months and 3 medications, reflecting the need in actual clinical practice for individualized homeopathic prescribing that often necessitates trying multiple remedies in order to achieve optimal results.

Despite some of the promising results described above, critics suggest that there is insufficient evidence to draw conclusions about the effectiveness of homeopathy for ADHD (Coulter & Dean, 2007) and studies are criticized as having methodological flaws (Rojas & Chan, 2005). The nature of homeopathy (selecting remedies for each individual based on numerous individual criteria) makes clinical trials for this modality a methodological challenge. Experts claim that homeopaths must have enough time to find a cure. Sometimes multiple remedies must be used in sequence and combination in order to optimize the healing process (Shalts, 2005). Because remedies are likely to be reasonably safe (Rojas & Chan, 2005), and anecdotal evidence suggests up to 70% success rate using homeopathic methods for at least 1 year (Brue & Oakland, 2002), additional work is called for to verify efficacy, and homeopathic treatment may be still be considered a viable alternative for treating ADHD.

Mind-Body Therapies: Meditation and Yoga

Meditation and yoga are both forms of mind-body practices, which elicit a relaxation response and reduce response to stress. Numerous forms of meditation exist, but all seek to cultivate mental and physiological calm through techniques that eliminate excessive thought.

Different techniques, originating from various spiritual traditions, use mantras, breath awareness, or movement to activate the parasympathetic nervous system, increase self-awareness, improve attention, and support emotional regulation. Research has explored the role of "neuroplasticity" in cognitive functioning, such as attention (Baijal & Gupta, 2008). Neuroplasticity refers to the phenomenon that the brain's functions can be altered through training and environmental experience. There is growing evidence for the beneficial effects of meditation-based training techniques for many conditions including anxiety disorders, depression, and chronic pain, among others. Meditation practice, which over time helps to quiet the mind, may even have a prophylactic effect, creating a calmer constitution that protects against circumstances that act as normal ADHD triggers.

Harrison, Manocha, and Rubia (2004) studied a form of meditation called Sahaja Yoga Meditation on core symptoms of ADHD using a family treatment model. The treatment program consisted of twice-weekly 90-minute sessions over a period of 6 weeks. Participants were taught to achieve a state of "thoughtless awareness," and were asked to meditate regularly at home. Results showed improvement in ADHD behavior, self-esteem, and relationship quality, and parents reported feeling happier, less stressed, and more able to manage their child's behavior. More recently, Zylowska et al. (2008) conducted a study on mindfulness meditation for ADHD and found promising results. Twenty-four adults and eight adolescents diagnosed with ADHD were involved in an 8-week training program in a modified version of mindfulness meditation. This technique involves bringing attention to an "anchor" such as breathing, noticing and letting go of distractions when they occur, and refocusing back on the anchor. Weekly sessions were supported by daily home practice. Seventy-eight percent of participants reported a reduction in total ADHD symptoms, with 30% reporting at least a 30% symptom reduction. Participants reported great satisfaction with the program and reductions in depressive and anxiety symptoms. On neurocognitive test performance, significant improvements were found on the measure of attentional conflict and on several other neuropsychological tests. The promising results and the absence of adverse events suggest meditation to be a helpful complement.

Yoga is an increasingly popular lifestyle practice often lauded for its therapeutic benefits for a range of health conditions, including conditions that often are associated with ADHD such as anxiety and oppositional defiant disorder. This ancient mind-body practice originating in India blends physical postures, breathing exercises, and meditation techniques. Little research has been conducted on yoga specifically for ADHD. In the only known study on yoga for ADHD (Jensen & Kenny, 2004), 14 boys with ADHD who were stabilized on medications completed either once-weekly yoga lessons or cooperative activities. Using a randomized crossover design, five of the control subjects crossed over to yoga at the end of the first 20-week period. (Therefore, 11 boys completed the yoga training and 8 boys acted as controls.) Subjects were assessed pre- and postintervention using the Connors Parent and Teacher Rating Scales, the Test of Variables of Attention, and the Motion Logger Actigraph. The yoga participants significantly improved their parent rating scores compared to the control group. These results suggest that yoga may have a role as an adjunct to conventional care (Rojas & Chan, 2005), although more research is needed.

Although meditation and yoga were presented here in the context of physical and mental practice, they have roots in spiritual traditions that also may contribute to their healing effect. In fact, the potential power of spiritual and religious practice should not be overlooked. Aiming to fulfill a "higher purpose," whatever it may be, can provide individuals with the focus and motivation to persist in completing a task and overcoming challenges even when biology offers stumbling blocks. An introspective search toward identifying one's personal purpose can help direct and sustain effective ADHD management.

Neurofeedback/EEG Biofeedback

Neurofeedback or electroencephalogram (EEG) biofeedback training uses visual or auditory cues to give subjects information about psychophysiologic processes (such as skin temperature or heart rate), which are generally out of the subject's immediate awareness. Research conducted over several decades now has demonstrated effectiveness for a broad range of mental and physical health conditions.

EEG biofeedback for children with ADHD is based upon the research findings that children with ADHD have higher levels of EEG abnormalities compared to controls. "Neurofeedback . . . relies on research that most people with ADHD, as compared with matched peers, have excess (theta) slow wave activity and reduced (beta) fast wave activity" (Sadiq, 2007, p. 513). EEG biofeedback training is used to normalize rhythms, thereby improving core symptoms such as hyperactivity and attention (Rojas & Chan, 2005).

A large body of evidence supports the use of biofeedback for ADHD. "Short-term effects were shown to be comparable to those of stimulants on the behavioral and neuropsychological level, leading to significant decreases of inattention, hyperactivity, and impulsivity" (Holtmann & Stadler, 2006, p. 533). In one study (Rossiter & LaVaque, 1995), EEG biofeedback and psychostimulants were compared in their efficacy with ADHD populations. As measured by a Continuous Performance Test (see Appendix B), both groups improved on measures of inattention, impulsivity, information processing, and variability. The authors deemed it an effective alternative to medication.

However, biofeedback research methodology often has been criticized for reasons such as lack of appropriate controls, failure to randomly allocate participants to treatment conditions, and small unequal sample sizes (Holtmann & Stadler, 2006). There are, of course, pros and cons for incorporating biofeedback into a treatment approach. Rojas and Chan (2005) point out that EEG biofeedback involves substantial cost and time, however "some families may prefer once or twice-weekly biofeedback sessions over daily medications and . . . some insurance companies may reimburse neurotherapy if prescribed by a physician" (p. 117).

Mother Nature

Lifestyle choices can play an important role in ADHD management. Some propose that even Mother Nature can be highly therapeutic. One study proposed that activities in green surroundings are "widely effective" in reducing symptoms associated with ADHD (Kuo & Taylor, 2004) although the methodology of this study has been criticized (Canu & Gordon, 2005). Nonetheless, a recommendation of daily exposure to green outdoor spaces seems at least harmless as part of a healthy lifestyle and as an adjunct to conventional ADHD treatment. Additionally, it is possible that there may even be optimal environments for different people. For example, some people experience greater calm, lower stress, and reduced restlessness near oceans and rivers, whereas others prefer lush mountainous regions.

Clearly, there are many alternative and complementary choices available to families of children with ADHD, most of which have few reported side effects. Although some are backed by significant bodies of evidence, more well-designed research studies are required before these modalities can be recommended as efficacious treatment alternatives to standard practice. Arnold (2002) notes that many alternative treatments target specific etiologies (such as nutritional deficiencies or sensitivities) and that a thorough history and physical exam should help check for signs of allergic history, food intolerance, dietary imbalances, mineral deficiencies, high lead levels, and general medical problems. This information can help determine the likelihood of success with various alternative and complementary modalities.

Conclusion

UNDERSTANDING the importance of attention and its impact on everyday living is essential to providing the most effective and comprehensive set of strategies, treatments, services, and programs for those individuals with ADHD. All stakeholders—parents, teachers, and professionals working with youngsters, adolescents, and adults—can together provide the necessary guidance and support that ensures success in school, at work, at home, and in the community.

This book is devoted to describing a comprehensive multimodal approach to addressing the needs of children and adolescents with attentional issues. Through teamwork, as presented in the multimodal, 12-point plan (see Chapter 5), readers are presented with a plan to promote school success and, hopefully, life success for kids with ADHD. Comprehensive parts of this multimodal plan range from the cutting edge in alternative, medical, technological, and educational strategies, and coaching approaches. We passionately believe that the information and tools provided within this book will significantly address the issues faced by individuals with attentional issues. We hope that you and the children, adolescents, or adults with ADHD you work with have benefited from our guidance.

Resources

Web Sites

The National Institute of Mental Health—http://www. nimh.nih.gov

U.S. Department of Education Office of Special Education and Rehabilitative Services—http://www.ed.gov/ about/offices/list/osers/index.html

Children and Adults with Attention-Deficit/Hyperactivity Disorder (CHADD)—http://www.chadd.org

Nemours—http://www.nemours.org

LD Online—http://www.ldonline.org

Attention Deficit Disorder Association (ADDA)—http:// www.add.org

National Center for Learning Disabilities—http://www. ncld.org

Learning Disabilities Association of America—http://www. ldaamerica.org

All Kinds of Minds—http://www.allkindsofminds.org

The REACH Institute—http://www.thereachinstitute.org

Council for Exceptional Children—http://www.cec.sped.org

Smart Kids with Learning Disabilities—http://www.smartkidswithld.org

Wrightslaw Libraries—http://www.wrightslaw.com

National Dissemination Center for Children With Disabilities—http://www.nichcy.org

National Resource Center on AD/HD—http://www.help4adhd.org

Parent Encouragement Program—http://www.parentencouragement.org

GreatSchools—http://www.greatschools.net

Information on Attention Deficit Disorder & ADHD—http://www.helpforadd.com/info

Recording for the Blind & Dyslexic—http://www.rfbd.org

ADDitude Magazine—http://www.additudemag.com/adhd-guide/adhd-at-school.html

Books

Bain, L. J. (1991). *A parent's guide to attention deficit disorders.* New York: Delta.

Barkley, R. A. (1991). *Attention-deficit hyperactivity disorder: A clinical workbook.* New York: Guilford.

Barkley, R. A. (2000). *Taking charge of ADHD: The complete, authoritative guide for parents.* New York: Guilford.

Bramer, J. S. (1996). *Succeeding in college with attention deficit disorders.* Plantation, FL: Specialty Press.

Caffrey, J. A. (1997). *First star I see.* Fairport, NY: Verbal Images.

Coloroso, B. (1994). *Kids are worth it!* Toronto, ON: Somerville House.

DuPaul, G. H., & Stoner, G. (1994). *ADHD in the school: Assessment and intervention strategies.* New York: Guilford.

Fowler, M. C. (1990). *Maybe you know my kid: A parent's guide to identifying, understanding and helping your child with ADHD.* New York: Birch Lane.

Galvin, M. (1995). *Otto learns about his medicine: A story about medicine for children with ADHD.* Washington, DC: Magination Press.

Gantos, J. (2000). *Joey Pigza loses control.* New York: Farrar, Straus & Giroux.

Gehret, J. (1991). *Eagle eyes: A child's guide to paying attention* (2nd ed.). Fairport, NY: Verbal Images Press.

Goldstein, S. G. (1995). *Understanding and managing children's classroom behavior.* New York: Wiley.

Goldstein, S., & Goldstein, M. (1993). *Hyperactivity: Why won't my child pay attention? A complete guide to ADD for parents, teachers, and community agencies.* New York: Wiley.

Hallowell, E. M., & Ratey, J. J. (1994). *Driven to distraction: Recognizing and coping with Attention Deficit Disorder from childhood to adulthood.* New York: Pantheon.

Janover, C. (1997). *Zipper, the kid with ADHD.* Bethesda, MD: Woodbine House.

Jensen, P. S. (2005). *Making the system work for your child with ADHD.* New York: Guilford.

Nadeau, K., Littman, E., & Quinn, P. (2000). *Understanding girls with AD/HD.* Silver Spring, MD: Advantage Books.

Nadeau, K. G., & Dixon, E. B. (1991). *Learning to slow down and pay attention.* Annandale, VA: Chesapeake Psychological Publications.

Nadeau, K. G., Dixon, E. B., & Biggs, S. (1993). *School strategies for ADD teens.* Annandale, VA: Chesapeake Psychological Publications.

Nemiroff, M. A., & Annunziata, J. (1998). *Help is on the way: A child's book about ADD.* Washington, DC: Magination Press.

Parker, H. C. (1992). *ADAPT teacher planbook.* Plantation, FL: Impact.

Parker, R. N. (1992). *Making the grade: An adolescent's struggle with ADD.* Plantation, FL: Impact.

Quinn, P. (1991). *Putting on the brakes: A child's guide to understanding and gaining control over attention deficit hyperactivity disorder* (ADHD). New York: Magination Press.

Smith, M. (1997). *Pay attention, Slosh!* Morton Grove, IL: Albert Whitman.

Weiss, G., & Hechtman, L. T. (1994). *Hyperactive children grown up* (2nd ed.). New York: Guilford.

Zimmert, D. (2001). *Eddie enough!* Bethesda, MD: Woodbine.

References

Abikoff, H. (2001). Tailored psychosocial treatments for ADHD: The search for a good fit. *Journal of Clinical Child Psychology, 30*, 122–125.

American Academy of Child & Adolescent Psychiatry. (2008). *ADHD—A guide for families*. Retrieved from http://www.aacap.org/cs/adhd_a_guide_for_families/how_common_is_adhd

American Academy of Pediatrics. (2001). Clinical practice guideline: Treatment of the school-aged child with Attention-Deficit/Hyperactivity Disorder. *Pediatrics, 108*, 1033–1044.

American Psychiatric Association. (2000). *Diagnostic and statistical manual of mental disorders, Text revision* (4th ed.; DSM-IV-TR). Washington, DC: American Psychiatric Association.

Anastopoulos, A., & Barkley, R. A. (1992). Attention deficit hyperactivity disorder. In C. E. Walker & M. Roberts (Eds.), *Handbook of clinical child psychology* (2nd ed., pp. 413–430). New York: Wiley.

Anastopoulos, A. D., Smith, J. M., & Wien, E. E. (1998). Counseling and training parents. In R. A. Barkley (Ed.), *Attention-deficit hyperactivity disorder: A handbook for diagnosis and treatment* (2nd ed., pp. 373–393). New York: Guilford.

Anderson, V. (1998). Assessing executive functions in children: Biological, psychological, and developmental considerations. *Neuropsychological Rehabilitation, 8,* 319–349.

Arnold, L. E., Chuang, S., Davies, M., Abikoff, H. B., Conners, C. K., Elliott, G. R., et al. (2004). Nine months of multicomponent behavioral treatment for ADHD and effectiveness of MTA fading procedures. *Journal of Abnormal Child Psychology, 32,* 39–51.

Arnold, L. E., Elliot, M., Sachs, L., Kraemer, H. C., Abikoff, H. B., Conners, C. K., et al. (2003). Attendance, stimulant response/dose, and 14-month outcome in ADHD. *Journal of Consulting and Clinical Psychology, 71,* 713–727.

Arnold, E. (2002). Treatment alternatives for attention deficit hyperactivity disorder. In P. S. Jensen & J. R. Cooper (Eds.), *Attention deficit hyperactivity disorder: State of the science-best practices* (pp. 13-1–13-29). Kingston, NJ: Civic Research Institute.

Attention Deficit Disorder Association Subcommittee on AD/HD Coaching. (2002). *The ADDA guiding principles for coaching individuals with attention deficit disorder.* Retrieved from http://www.add.org/articles/coachinguide.html

Attention Deficit Disorder/Attention Deficit Hyperactivity Disorder. (n.d.). Retrieved October 27, 2008, from http://www.attentiondeficitadd.com

Baijal, S., & Gupta, R. (2008). Meditation-based training: A possible intervention for attention deficit hyperactivity disorder? *Psychiatry, 5*(4), 48–55.

Barkley, R. A. (n.d.). *About ADHD—A fact sheet by Dr. Barkley.* Retrieved November 6, 2008, from http://www.russellbarkley.org/adhd-facts.htm#othercharacteristics

Barkley, R. A. (1987). *Defiant children: A clinician's manual for parent training.* New York: Guilford.

Barkley, R. A. (1990). *Attention deficit hyperactivity disorder: A handbook for diagnosis and treatment.* New York: Guilford.

Barkley, R. A. (1997a). *ADHD and the nature of self-control.* New York: Guilford.

Barkley, R. A. (1997b). Behavioral inhibition, sustained attention, and executive functions: Constructing a unifying theory of ADHD. *Psychological Bulletin, 121,* 65–94.

Barkley, R. A. (1997c). *Defiant children: A clinician's manual for assessment and parent training* (2nd ed.). New York: Guilford.

Barkley, R. A. (1998). Attention-deficit hyperactivity disorder. *Scientific American, 279,* 66–71.

Barkley, R. A. (2000a). Genetics of childhood disorders: XVII. ADHD, Part I: The executive functions and ADHD. *Journal of the American Academy of Child & Adolescent Psychiatry, 39,* 1064–1070.

Barkley, R. A. (2000b). *Taking charge of ADHD: The complete, authoritative guide for parents,* New York: Guilford.

Barkley, R. A. (2003). Attention-deficit/hyperactivity disorder. In E. J. Mash & R. A. Barkley (Eds.), *Child psychopathology* (2nd ed., pp. 75–143). New York: Guilford.

Barkley, R. A. (2005). *ADHD and the nature of self-control* (Rev. ed.). New York: Guilford.

Barkley, R. A. (2006). *Attention deficit hyperactivity disorder: A handbook for diagnosis and treatment* (3rd ed.). New York: Guilford.

Barkley, R. A. (2007). *ADHD in adults: What the science says.* New York: Guilford.

Barkley, R. A. Edwards, G., Laneri, M., Fletcher, K., & Metevia, L. (2001). Executive functioning, temporal discounting, and sense of time in adolescents with attention deficit hyperactivity disorder and oppositional defiant disorder. *Journal of Abnormal Child Psychology, 29,* 541–556.

Barkley, R. A., Fischer, M., Edelbrock, C. S., & Smallish, L. (1990). The adolescent outcome of hyperactive children diagnosed by research criteria: An 8-year prospective follow-up study. *Journal of the American Academy of Child & Adolescent Psychiatry, 29,* 546–557.

Barkley, R. A., Koplowitz, S., Anderson, T., & McMurray, M. B. (1997). Sense of time in children with ADHD: Effects of duration, distraction, and stimulant medication. *Journal of the International Neuropsychological Society, 3*, 359–369.

Barkley, R. A., & Murphy, K. R. (2006). *Attention-deficit hyperactivity disorder: A clinical workbook* (3rd ed.). New York: Guilford Press.

Barnes, P., Powell-Griner, E., McFann, K., & Nahin, R. (2004). Complementary and alternative medicine use among adults: United States, 2002. *Advanced Data, 27*(343), 1–19.

Baron-Cohen, S. (2000). Is Asperger's syndrome/high-functioning autism necessarily a disability? *Development and Psychopathology, 12*, 489–500.

Biederman, J., Faraone, S., Milberger, S., Guite, J., Mick, E., Chen, L., et al. (1996). A prospective 4-year follow-up of attention-deficit hyperactivity and related disorders. *Archives of General Psychiatry, 53*, 437–446.

Biederman, J., Mick, E., Faraone, S. V., Braaten, E., Doyle, A., Spencer, T., et al. (2002). Influence of gender on Attention Deficit Hyperactivity Disorder in children referred to a psychiatric clinic. *American Journal of Psychiatry. 159*(1), 36–42.

Boschert, S. (2008). Behavioral treatment can delay initiation of ADHD medication. *Clinical Psychiatry News, 36*(9), 1, 6.

Bradley, C. (1937). The behavior of children receiving benzedrine. *American Journal of Psychiatry, 94*, 577–585.

Bradley, C., & Bowen, M. (1940). School performance of children receiving amphetamine (benzedrine) sulfate. *American Journal of Orthopsychiatry, 10*, 782–788.

Brown, T. E. (n.d.). *The Brown model of ADD syndrome.* Retrieved November 11, 2008, from http://www.drthomasebrown.com/brown_model/index.html

Brown, T. E. (2005). *Attention deficit disorder: The unfocused mind in children and adults.* New Haven, CT: Yale University Press.

Brue, A. W., & Oakland, T. D. (2002). Alternative treatments for attention-deficit/hyperactivity disorder: Does evidence support their use? *Alternative Therapies in Health and Medicine, 8*(1), 68–74.

Butnik, S. M. (2005). Neurofeedback in adolescents and adults with attention-deficit/hyperactivity disorder. *Journal of Clinical Psychology, 61*, 621–625.

Canu, W., & Gordon, M. (2005). Mother nature as treatment for ADHD: Overstating the benefits of green. *American Journal of Public Health, 95,* 371.

Chan, E. (2002). The role of complementary and alternative medicine in attention-deficit hyperactivity disorder. *Journal of Developmental and Behavioral Pediatrics, 23,* S37–S45.

Chan, E., Rappaport, L. A., & Kemper, K. J. (2003). Complementary and alternative therapies in childhood attention and hyperactivity problems. *Journal of Developmental and Behavioral Pediatrics, 24,* 4–8.

Children and Adults with Attention Deficit Hyperactivity Disorder. (n.d.). *Locate the CHADD chapter nearest you.* Retrieved November 11, 2008, from http://www.chadd.org/AM/Template.cfm?Section=Find_Local_CHADD_Chapters&Template=/CustomPages/ChapterLocator/findchap.cfm

Children and Adults with Attention Deficit Hyperactivity Disorder. (2003a). *Succeeding in college.* Retrieved from http://www.help4adhd.org/education/college/wwk13

Children and Adults with Attention Deficit Hyperactivity Disorder. (2003b). *Succeeding in the workplace.* Retrieved from http://www.help4adhd.org/living/workplace/wwk16

Cogmed Working Memory Training. (n.d.). *Welcome to Cogmed.* Retrieved November 3, 2008, from http://www.cogmed.com

Conners, C. K. (1997). *Conners' rating scales–Revised.* North Tonawanda, NY: Multi-Health Systems.

Conners, C. K. (2000). *Conners' continuous performance test II, Version 5.* North Tonawanda, NY: Multi-Health Systems.

Conners, C. K., Epstein, J., & March, J. (2001). Multimodal treatment of ADHD (MTA): An alternative outcome analysis. *Journal of the American Academy of Child & Adolescent Psychiatry, 40,* 159–167.

Connor, D. F., & Meltzer, B. M. (2006). *Pediatric psychopharmacology: Fast facts.* New York: W. W. Norton.

Coulter, M. K., & Dean, M. E. (2007). Homeopathy for attention deficit/hyperactivity disorder or hyperkinetic disorder. (Cochrane Database of Systematic Reviews No. CD005648)

Curtis, L. T., & Patel, K. (2008). Nutritional and environmental approaches to preventing and treating autism and attention deficit hyperactivity disorder (ADHD): A review. *Journal of Alternative and Complementary Medicine, 14,* 79–85.

Delis, D. C., Kaplan, E., & Kramer, J. H. (2001). *Delis-Kaplan executive function system (D-KEFS).* Upper Saddle River, NJ: Pearson.

Demaray, M. K., Schaefer, K., & DeLong, L. (2003). Attention-deficit/hyperactivity disorder (ADHD): A national survey of training and current assessment practices in the schools. *Psychology in the Schools, 40,* 583–597.

Dendy, C. A. Z. (2000). *Teaching teens with ADD and ADHD: A quick reference guide for teachers and parents.* Bethesda, MD: Woodbine House.

Dendy, C. A. Z. (Ed.). (2006). *CHADD educator's manual on attention deficit/hyperactivity disorder (AD/HD): An in-depth look from an educational perspective.* Landover, MD: CHADD.

Dendy, C. A. Z., & Zeigler, A. (2003). *A bird's-eye view of life with ADD and ADHD.* Cedar Bluff, AL: Cherish the Children.

DiScala, C., Lescohier, I., Barthel, M., & Li, G. (1998). Injuries to children with attention deficit hyperactivity disorder. *Pediatrics, 102,* 1415–1421.

Döpfner, M., Breuer, D., Schürmann, S., Metternich, T. W., Rademacher, C., Lehmkuhl, G. (2004). Effectiveness of an adaptive multimodal treatment in children with attention-deficit hyperactivity disorder—Global outcome. *European Child and Adolescent Psychiatry, 13,* I117–I129.

Douglas, C. A., & Morley, W. H. (2000). *Executive coaching: An annotated bibliography.* Greensboro, NC: Center for Creative Leadership

DuPaul, G. J., & Eckert, T. L. (1997). The effects of school-based intervention for attention deficit hyperactivity disorder: A meta-analysis. *School Psychology Review, 26,* 5–27.

DuPaul, G. J., & Eckert, T. L. (1998). Academic interventions for students with attention-deficit/hyperactivity disorder: A review of the literature. *Reading and Writing Quarterly: Overcoming Learning Disabilities, 14,* 59–82. (ERIC Document Reproduction Service No. EJ590993)

DuPaul, G. J., Power, T. J., Anastopoulos, A. D., & Reid, R. (1998). *ADHD rating scale IV.* New York: Guilford.

DuPaul, G. J., & Stoner, G. (2002). Interventions for attention problems. In M. Shinn, H. M. Walker, & G. Stoner (Eds.), *Interventions for academic and behavioral problems II: Preventive and remedial approaches* (pp. 913–938). Bethesda, MD: National Association of School Psychologists.

Edwards, M. C., Gardner, E. S., Chelonis, J. J., Schulz, E. G., Flake, R. A., & Diaz, P. F. (2007). Estimates of the validity and utility of the Conners' Continuous Performance Test in the assessment of inattentive and/or hyperactive-impulsive behaviors in children. *Journal of Abnormal Child Psychology, 35*, 393–404.

Edwards, M. C., Schulz, E. G., Chelonis, J., Gardner, E., Philyaw, A., & Young, J. (2005). Estimates of the validity and utility of unstructured clinical observations of children in the assessment of ADHD. *Clinical Pediatrics, 44*, 49–56.

Eisenberg, D. T., Campbell, B., Gray, P. B., & Sorenson, M. D. (2008). Dopamine receptor genetic polymorphisms and body composition in undernourished pastoralists: An exploration of nutrition indices among nomadic and recently settled Ariaal men of northern Kenya. *BMC Evolutionary Biology, 8*, 173.

Eisenberg, D. M., Davis, R. B., Ettner, S. L., Appel, S. M., Wilkey, S. A., Van Rompay, M. I. et al. (1998). Trends in alternative medicine use in the United States, 1990–1997. *Journal of the American Medical Association, 280*, 1569–1575.

Faraone, S. V., & Kunwar, A. (2007). *ADHD in children with comorbid conditions: Diagnosis, misdiagnosis, and keeping tabs on both.* Retrieved from http://www.medscape.com/viewarticle/555748

Feingold, B. F. (1975). Hyperkinesis and learning disabilities linked to artificial food flavors and colors. *American Journal of Nursing, 75*, 797–803.

Finn, C. A., & Sladeczek, I. E. (2001). Assessing the social validity of behavioral interventions: A review of treatment acceptability measures. *School Psychology Quarterly, 16*, 176–206.

Fisher, B. C. (2006). *Attention deficit disorder: Practical coping mechanisms.* New York: Informa HealthCare.

Foley Nicpon, M., Wodrich, D. L., & Robinson Kurpius, S. E. (2004). Utilization behavior in boys with ADHD: A test of Barkley's theory. *Journal of Developmental Neuropsychology, 26*, 735–751.

Forehand, R. L., & McMahon, R. J. (1981). *Helping the noncompliant child: A clinician's guide to parent training.* New York: Guilford Press.

Foy, J. M., & Earls, M. F. (2005). A process for developing community consensus regarding the diagnosis and management of attention-deficit/ hyperactivity disorder. *Pediatrics, 115,* E97–E104.

Freeman, M. P., Hibbeln, J. R., Wisner, K. L., Davis, J. M., Mischoulon, D., Peet, M., et al. (2006). Omega-3 fatty acids: Evidence basis for treatment and future research in psychiatry. *Journal of Clinical Psychiatry, 67,* 1954–1967.

Frei, H., Everts, R., von Ammon, K., Kaufmann, F., Walther, D., Schmitz, S. F. (2007). Randomised controlled trials of homeopathy in hyperactive children: Treatment procedure leads to an unconventional study design. Experience with open-label homeopathic treatment preceding the Swiss ADHD placebo controlled, randomised, double-blind, cross-over trial. *Homeopathy: The Journal of the Faculty of Homeopathy, 96*(1), 35–41.

Gioia, G. A., Isquith, P. K., Guy, S. C., & Kenworthy, L. (2000). Behavior rating of executive function. Lutz, FL: Psychological Assessment Resources.

Goldberg, E., & Podell, K. (1995). Lateralization in the frontal lobes. In H. H. Jasper, S. Riggio, & P. S. Goldman-Rakic (Eds.), *Epilepsy and the functional anatomy of the frontal lobe* (pp. 85–96). New York: Raven Press.

Goldstein, S. (2000). *From assessment to treatment: Developing a comprehensive plan to help your child with ADHD.* Retrieved from http://www.addresources.org/article_adhd_assessment_treatment_goldstein.php

Graham, P., Rutter, M., & George, S. (1973). Temperamental characteristics as predictors of behavior disorders in children. *American Journal of Orthopsychiatry, 43,* 328–339.

Greene, R. W. (2001). *The explosive child.* New York: HarperCollins.

Greene, R. W. (1995). Students with ADHD in school classrooms: Teacher factors related to compatibility, assessment, and intervention. *School Psychology Review, 24,* 81–93.

Greene, R. W., & Ablon, J. S. (2001). What does the MTA study tell us about effective psychosocial treatment for ADHD? *Journal of Clinical Child and Adolescent Psychology, 30,* 114–121.

Greene, S. M., Loeber, R., & Lahey, B. B., (1991). Stability of mothers' recall of the age of onset of their child's attention and hyperactivity problems. *Journal of the American Academy of Child & Adolescent Psychiatry, 30,* 135–137.

Greenwood, C. R., Delquardi, J., & Carta, J. J. (1988). *Classwide peer tutoring.* Seattle, WA: Educational Achievement Systems.

Greenwood, C. R., Maheady, L., & Carta, J. J. (1991). Peer tutoring programs in the regular education classroom. In G. Stoner, M. R. Shinn, & H. M. Walker (Eds.), *Interventions for achievement and behavior problems* (p.179–200). Silver Spring, MD: National Association of School Psychologists.

Harrison, L. J., Manocha, R., & Rubia, K. (2004). Sahaja yoga meditation as a family treatment programme for children with attention deficit-hyperactivity disorder. *Clinical Child Psychology and Psychiatry, 9,* 479–497.

Hartmann, T. (1993). *Attention deficit disorder: A different perception.* Nevada City, CA: Underwood Books.

Hazelwood, E., Bovingdon, T., & Tiemens, K. (2002). The meaning of a multimodal approach for children with ADHD: Experience of service professionals. *Child Care, Health and Development, 28,* 301–307.

Heacox, D. (1991). *Up from underachievement: How teachers, students, and parents can work together to promote student success.* Minneapolis, MN: Free Spirit.

Hecker, L., Burns, L., Katz, L., Elkind, J., & Elkind, K. (2002). Benefits of assistive reading software for students with attention disorders. *Annals of Dyslexia, 52,* 243–272.

Hechtman, L., Etcovitch, J., Platt, R., Arnold, L. E., Abikoff, H. B., Newcorn, J. H., et al. (2005). Does multimodal treatment of ADHD decrease other diagnoses? *Clinical Neuroscience Research, 5,* 273–282.

Hinshaw, S. P. (1994). *Attention deficits and hyperactivity in children.* London: Sage.

Holtmann, M., & Stadler, C. (2006). Electroencephalographic biofeedback for the treatment of attention-deficit hyperactivity disorder in childhood and adolescence. *Expert Review of Neurotherapeutics, 6,* 533–540.

Hoza, B. (2001). Psychosocial treatment issues in the MTA: A reply to Greene and Ablon. *Journal of Clinical Child Psychology, 30*, 126–30.

Hoza, B., Mrug, S., Pelham, W. E., Jr., Greiner, A. R., & Gnagy, E. M. (2003). A friendship intervention for children with attention deficit/hyperactivity disorder: Preliminary findings. *Journal of Attention Disorders, 6,* 87–98.

Individuals with Disabilities Education Improvement Act, 34 CFR C.F.R. §300 and 301 (2006).

Jacobsen, M. F., & Schardt, D. (1999). *Diet, ADHD and behavior: A quarter-century review.* Washington, DC: Center for Science in the Public Interest.

Jenkins, S. (2008, Aug. 17). A fitting end to an emotional triumph. *The Washington Post*, D1, D12.

Jensen, P. S. (2005, Oct.). *Do children with ADHD get better? An MTA perspective.* Presented at the 52nd Annual Meeting of the American Academy of Child and Adolescent Psychiatry, Toronto, Canada.

Jensen, P. S., Garcia, J. A., Glied, S., Crowe, M., Foster, M., & Schlander, M. (2005). Cost-effectiveness of ADHD treatments: Findings from the multimodal treatment study of children with ADHD. *American Journal of Psychiatry, 162*, 1628–1636.

Jensen P. S., & Kenny, D. T. (2004). The effects of yoga on the attention and behavior of boys with attention-deficit/hyperactivity disorder (ADHD). *Journal of Attention Disorders, 7*, 205–216

Jeweler, S., Barnes-Robinson, L., Roffman Shevitz, B., & Weinfeld, R. (2008). Bordering on excellence: A teaching tool for twice-exceptional students. *Gifted Child Today, 32*(2), 40–46.

Johnston, C., & Mash, E. J. (2001). Families of children with attention-deficit/ hyperactivity disorder: Review and recommendations for future research. *Clinical Child and Family Psychology Review, 4*, 183–207.

Kagan, J. (1997). Temperament and the reactions to unfamiliarity. *Child Development, 68*, 139–144.

Kemner, J. E., Starr, H. L., Ciccone, P. E., Hooper-Wood, C. G., & Crockett, R. S. (2005). Outcomes of OROS methylphenidate compared with atomoxetine in children with ADHD: A multicenter, randomized prospective study. *Advances in Therapy, 22,* 498–512.

Kerns, K. A., & Price, K. J. (2001). An investigation of prospective memory in children with ADHD. *Child Neuropsychology, 7,* 162–171.

Klein, R. G., & Manuzza, S. (1991). The long-term outcome of hyperactive children: A review. *Journal of the American Academy of Child and Adolescent Psychiatry, 30,* 383–387.

Konofal, E., Lecendreux, M., Deron, J., Marchand, M., Cortese, S., & Zaim, M. (2008). Effects of iron supplementation on attention deficit hyperactivity disorder in children. *Pediatric Neurology, 38,* 20–26.

Kratochvil, C. J., Heiligenstein, J. H., Dittmann, R., Spencer, T. J., & Biederman, J. (2002). Methylphenidate treatment in children with ADHD: A prospective, randomized, open-label trial. *Journal of the American Academy of Child & Adolescent Psychiatry, 41,* 776–784.

Kuo, F. E., & Taylor, A. F. (2004). A potential natural treatment for attention-deficit/hyperactivity disorder: Evidence from a national study. *American Journal of Public Health, 94,* 1580–1586.

Kurzweil Educational Systems. (2006). *Kurzweil 3000—Solutions for struggling readers.* Retrieved from http://www.kurzweiledu.com/kurz3000. aspx

Lamont, J. (1997). Homeopathic treatment of attention-deficit disorder. *The British Homeopathic Journal, 86,* 196–200.

Laucht, M., Skowronek, M. H., Becker, K., Schmidt, M. H., Esser, G., Schulze, T. G., et al. (2007). Interacting effects of the dopamine transporter gene and psychosocial adversity on attention-deficit/hyperactivity disorder symptoms among 15-year-olds from a high-risk community sample. *Archives of General Psychiatry, 64,* 585–590.

Leibson, C. L., Katusic, S. K., Barbaresi, W. J., Ransom, J., & O'Brien, P. C. (2001). Use and cost of medical care for children and adolescents with and without attention-deficit/hyperactivity disorder. *Journal of the American Medical Association, 285,* 60–66.

Lenz, K., & Schumaker, J. (1999). *Adapting language arts, social studies, and science materials for the inclusive classroom: Volume 3: Grades six through eight.* Reston, VA: Council for Exceptional Children.

Lesesne, C., Abramowitz, A., Perou, R., & Brann, E. (2000). *Attention-deficit/ hyperactivity disorder: A public health research agenda: Center for Disease Control and Prevention.* Retrieved from http://www.cdc.gov/ncbddd/ adhd/dadagenda.htm

Lezak, M. D. (1995). *Neuropsychological assessment.* New York: Oxford University Press.

Loo, S. K., & Barkley, R. A. (2005). Clinical utility of EEG in attention deficit hyperactivity disorder. *Applied Neuropsychology, 12*(2), 64–76.

Low, K. (2008). *Michael Phelps: Making a splash.* Retrieved from http://add. about.com/b/2008/08/03/michael-phelps-making-a-splash-with-adhd. htm

Lubar, J. F., Swartwood, M. O., Swartwood, J. N., & O'Donnell, P. H. (1995). Evaluation of the effectiveness of EEG neurofeedback training for ADHD in a clinical setting as measured by changes in TOVA scores, behavioral ratings, and WISC-R performance. *Biofeedback and Self-Regulation, 20,* 83–99.

Lyon, M. R. & Cline, J. C., Totosy de Zepetnek, J., Shan, J. J., Pang, P., & Benishin, C. (2001). Effect of the herbal extract combination Panax quinquefolium and Ginkgo biloba on attention-deficit hyperactivity disorder: A pilot study. *Journal of Psychiatry and Neuroscience, 26,* 221–228.

Manuzza, S., Klein, R. G., Bessler, A., Malloy, P., & Lapadula, M. (1993). Adult outcome of hyperactive boys: Educational achievement, occupational rank, and psychiatric status. *Archives of General Psychiatry, 50,* 565–576.

Manuzza, S., Klein, R. G., Truong, N. L., Moulton, J. L. III, Roizen, E. R., Howell, K. H. et al. (2008). Age of methylphenidate treatment initiation in children with ADHD and later substance abuse: Prospective follow-up into adulthood. *American Journal of Psychiatry, 165,* 604–609.

Maryland State Department of Education. (1999). *Maryland state performance assessment program.* Baltimore: Author

McGoey, K. E., Eckert, T. L., & DuPaul, G. J. (2002). Early intervention for preschool-age children with ADHD: A literature review. *Journal of Emotional & Behavioral Disorders, 10,* 14–29.

McIntyre, T. (2004). *Strategies for teaching youth with ADD and ADHD.* Retrieved from http://www.ldonline.org/article/13701

Milazzo-Sayre, L. J., Henderson, M. J., Manderscheid, R. W., Bokossa, M. C., Evans, C., & Male, A. A. (2001). Persons treated in specialty mental health care programs, United States, 1997. In R. W. Manderscheid & M. J. Henderson (Eds.), *Mental health, United States, 2000* (pp. 172–217). Washington, DC: U.S. Government Printing Office. (DHHS Pub. No. (SMA) 01-3537)

Mori, L., & Peterson, L. (1995). Knowledge of safety of high and low active-impulsive boys: Implications for child injury prevention. *Journal of Clinical Child Psychology, 24,* 370–376.

Mousain-Bosc, M., Roche, M., Polge, A., Pradal-Prat, D., Rapin, J., & Bali, J. P. (2006). Improvement of neurobehavioral disorders in children supplemented with magnesium-vitamin B6. I. Attention deficit hyperactivity disorders. *Magnesium Research, 19,* 46–52.

Murray, D. W., Rabiner, D., Schulte, A., & Newitt, K. (2008). Feasibility and integrity of a parent-teacher consultation intervention for ADHD students. *Child & Youth Care Forum, 37,* 111–126.

Naglieri, J. A., Goldstein, S., Delauder, B. Y., & Schwebach, A. (2005). Relationships between the WISC-III and the Cognitive Assessment System with Conners' rating scales and continuous performance tests. *Archives of Clinical Neuropsychology, 20,* 385–401.

Naglieri, J. A., Goldstein, S., Iseman, J. S., & Schwebach, A. (2003). Performance of children with attention deficit hyperactivity disorder and anxiety/depression on the WISC-III and Cognitive Assessment System (CAS). *Journal of Psychoeducational Assessment, 21,* 32–42.

National Institute of Mental Health. (2008a). *Attention deficit hyperactivity disorder in adults.* Retrieved from http://www.nimh.nih.gov/health/publications/adhd/attention-deficit-hyperactivity-disorder-in-adults.shtml

National Institute of Mental Health. (2008b). *Diagnosis.* Retrieved from http://www.nimh.nih.gov/health/publications/adhd/diagnosis.html

National Institute of Mental Health. (2008c). *Disorders that sometimes accompany ADHD.* Retrieved from http://www.nimh.nih.gov/health/publications/adhd/disorders-that-sometimes-accompany-adhd.shtml

New research: ADHD medication use growing faster among adults than children. (n.d.). Retrieved November 6, 2008, from http://phx.corporate-ir.net/ phoenix.zhtml?c=131268&p=irol-newsArticle&ID=756843&highlight=

Palmer, E. D., & Finger, S. (2001). An early description of ADHD (inattentive subtype): Dr. Alexander Crichton and "mental restlessness" (1798). *Child and Adolescent Mental Health, 6*(2), 66–73.

Pelham, W. E., & Murphy, H. A. (1986). Attention deficit and conduct disorders. In M. Hersen (Ed.), *Pharmacological and behavioral treatment: An integrative approach* (pp. 108–148). New York: Wiley.

Pelham, W. E., Wheeler, T., & Chronis, A. (1998). Empirically supported psychosocial treatments for attention deficit hyperactivity disorder. *Journal of Clinical Child Psychology, 27*, 190–205.

Pfeiffer, S. I., Reddy, L. A., Kletzel, J. E., Schmelzer, E. R., & Boyer, L. M. (2000). The practitioner's view of IQ testing and profile analysis. *School Psychology Quarterly, 15*, 376–385.

Pfiffner, L. J., & Barkley, R. A. (1990). Educational placement and classroom management. In R. A. Barkley (Ed.), *Attention deficit hyperactivity disorder: A handbook for diagnosis and treatment* (pp. 498–539). New York: Guilford.

Play Attention. (2007). *Play Attention's benefits.* Retrieved from http://www. playattention.com/solution

Pliszka, S., & AACAP Work Group on Quality Issues. (2007). Practice parameter for the assessment and treatment of children and adolescents with attention-deficit/hyperactivity disorder. *Journal of the American Academy of Child & Adolescent Psychiatry, 46*, 894–921.

Pribram, K. H. (1976). Executive functions of the frontal lobes. In T. Desiraju (Ed.), *Mechanisms in transmission of signals of conscious behaviour.* Amsterdam: Elsevier

Pribram, K. H., & McGuinness, D. (1975). Arousal, activation, and effort in the control of attention. *Psychological Review, 82*, 116–149.

Quinn, P. O., Ratey, N. A., & Maitland, T. I (2001). Working with an ADD coach. In P. O. Quinn (Ed.), *ADD and the college student: A guide for high school and college students with attention deficit disorder* (p. 99–109). Washington, DC: Magination Press.

Rabiner, D. (n.d.). *Using a home-school report card with your ADHD child.* Retrieved October 29, 2008, from http://www.addresources.org/article_adhd_home_school_report_rabiner.php

Rapport, M. D., Chung, K.-M., Shore, G., Denney, C. B., & Isaacs, P. (2000). Upgrading the science and technology of assessment and diagnosis: Laboratory and clinic-based assessment of children with ADHD. *Journal of Clinical Child Psychology, 29,* 555–568.

Reid, R., & Maag, J. (1998). Functional assessment: A method for developing classroom-based accommodations for children with ADHD. *Reading and Writing Quarterly, 14,* 9–42.

Reid, R., Vasa, S. F., Maag, J. W., & Wright, G. (1994). Who are the children with ADHD: A school-based survey. *Journal of Special Education, 28,* 117–137.

Renzulli, J. S. (1977). *The enrichment triad model: A guide for developing defensible programs for the gifted and talented.* Mansfield Center, CT: Creative Learning Press.

Reynolds, C. R., & Kamphaus, R. W. (2004). *BASC-2: Behavior assessment system for children* (2nd ed.). Upper Saddle River, NJ: Pearson/AGS.

Ricci, M. C., Barnes-Robinson, L., & Jeweler, S. (2006, Sept.). Helping your children build on their visual-spatial strength in a world of words. *Parenting for High Potential,* 5–7, 30.

Robertson, M. M. (2000). Tourette syndrome, associated conditions and the complexities of treatment. *Brain, 123,* 425–462.

Robin, A. L. (n.d.). *Helping your adolescent with ADHD get homework done.* Retrieved from http://www.add.org/articles/teenhomework.html

Rojas, N. L., & Chan, E. (2005). Old and new controversies in the alternative treatment of attention-deficit hyperactivity disorder. *Mental Retardation and Developmental Disabilities Research Reviews, 11,* 116–130.

Rossiter, T. R., & La Vaque, T. J. (1995). A comparison of EEG biofeedback and psychostimulants in treating attention deficit/hyperactivity disorders. *Journal of Neurotherapy, 1,* 48–59.

Rossiter, T. (2004). The effectiveness of neurofeedback and stimulant drugs in treating AD/HD: Part II. Replication. *Applied Psychophysiology and Biofeedback, 29,* 233–243.

Rowe, R., Maughan, B., & Goodman, R. (2004). Childhood psychiatric disorder and unintentional injury: Findings from a national cohort study. *Journal of Pediatric Psychology, 29,* 119–130.

Rubia, K. (2002). The dynamic approach to neurodevelopmental psychiatric disorders: Use of fMRI combined with neuropsychology to elucidate the dynamics of psychiatric disorders, exemplified in ADHD and schizophrenia. *Behavioural Brain Research, 130,* 47–56.

Sadiq, A. (2007). Attention-deficit/hyperactivity disorder and integrative approaches. *Pediatric Annals, 36,* 508–515.

Sanford, J. (2008). *What is brain training and cognitive rehabilitation?* Retrieved from http://www.braintrain.com/main/what-is-brain-training.htm

Scahill, L., Schwab-Stone, M., Merikangas, K. R., Leckman, J. F., Zhang, H., & Kasl, S. (1999). Psychosocial and clinical correlates of ADHD in a community sample of school-age children. *Journal of the American Academy of Child & Adolescent Psychiatry, 38,* 976–984.

Schaughency, E. A., & Rothlind, J. (1991). Assessment and classification of attention-deficit hyperactivity disorders. *School Psychology Review, 20,* 187–202.

Schmidt, M. H., Möcks, P., Lay, B., Eisert, H. G., Fojkar, R., Fritz-Sigmund, D., et al. (1997). Does oligoantigenic diet influence hyperactive/conduct-disordered children?—A controlled study. *European Child & Adolescent Psychiatry, 6,* 88–95.

Schusteff, A. (n.d.). *Preschool-age ADHD children: Too young for a diagnosis?* Retrieved July 4, 2008, from http://www.additudemag.com/adhd/article/2488.html

Section 504 of the Rehabilitation Act, 29 U.S.C. Section 706 et. Seq. (1973).

Shalts, E. (2005). *The American Institute of Homeopathy handbook for parents.* Hoboken, NJ: Wiley.

Silverman, S. M., & Weinfeld, R. (2007). *School success for kids with Asperger's syndrome.* Waco, TX: Prufrock Press.

Singh Maharaj, S. R. (2000, Dec.). Bringing peace through spirituality and meditation to zones of conflict. *Sat Sandesh: The Message of the Science of Spirituality, 2*

Smith, K. G., & Corkum, P. (2007). Systematic review of measures used to diagnose attention-deficit/hyperactivity disorder in research on preschool children. *Topics in Early Childhood Special Education, 27,* 164–173.

Society of Nuclear Medicine. (2003). 123-Altropane SPECT show potential as diagnostic tool for ADHD. Retrieved from http://www.scienceblog. com

Sohlberg, M. M., & Mateer, C. A. (1989). *Introduction to cognitive rehabilitation: Theory and practice.* New York: Guilford.

Stevens, L. J., & Zentall, T. (1996). Omega-3 fatty acids in boys with behavior, learning and health problems. *Physiology & Behavior, 59,* 915–920.

Stubberfield, T. G., Wray, T. A., & Parry, T. S. (1999). Utilization of alternative therapies in attention-deficit hyperactivity disorder. *Journal of Pediatrics and Child Health, 35,* 450–453.

Swanson, J. M., Greenhill, L. L., Lopez, F. A., Sedillo, A., Earl, C. Q., Jiang, J. G., et al. (2006). Modafinil film-coated tablets in children and adolescents with attention-deficit/hyperactivity disorder: Results of a randomized, double-blind, placebo-controlled, fixed-dose study followed by abrupt discontinuation. *Journal of Clinical Psychiatry, 67,* 137–147.

Swanson, J. M., McBurnett, K., & Wigal, T. (1993). Effect of stimulant medication on children with attention-deficit disorder—A review of reviews. *Exceptional Children, 60,* 154–162

Swartz, S. L., Prevatt, F., & Proctor, B. E. (2005). A coaching intervention for college students with attention deficit/hyperactivity disorder. *Psychology in the Schools, 42,* 647–656.

Todd, R. D., Sitdhiraksa, N., Reich, W., Ji, T., Joyner, C., Heath, A. C. et al. (2002). Discrimination of DSM-IV and latent class attention-deficit/ hyperactivity disorder subtypes by educational and cognitive performance in a population-based sample of child and adolescent twins. *Journal of the American Academy of Child and Adolescent Psychiatry, 41,* 820–828.

Tomlinson, C. A. (1999). *Differentiated classrooms—One pathway to a new millennium.* Albuquerque, NM: National Association for Gifted Children.

Toplak, M. E., Connors, L., Shuster, J., Knezevic, B., & Parks, S. (2008). Review of cognitive, cognitive-behavioral, and neural-based interventions for attention-deficit/hyperactivity disorder (ADHD). *Clinical Psychology Review, 28,* 801–823.

Trebaticka, J., Kopasova, S., Hradecna, Z., Cinovsky, K., Skodacek, I., Suba, J. et al. (2006). Treatment of ADHD with French maritime pine bark extract, Pycnogenol. *European Child & Adolescent Psychiatry, 15*, 329–335.

Trout, A. L., Ortiz Lienemann, T., Reid, R., & Epstein, M. H. (2007). A review of non-medication interventions to improve the academic performance of children and youth with ADHD. *Remedial & Special Education, 28*, 207–226.

Turkelson, C. M., Goldstein, L.A., Doggett, D., Mitchell, M. D., & Tregear, S. (2000). Continuous performance tests (CPTs) for diagnosis and titration of medication for attention deficit hyperactivity disorder (ADHD): Full health care technology assessment. Retrieved from http://www. ablechild.org/right%20to%20refuse/continuous_performance_tests.htm

U.S. Department of Education. (2004). *Teaching children with attention deficit hyperactivity disorder: Instructional strategies and practices.* Retrieved from http://www.ldonline.org/article/8797

U.S. Department of Health and Human Resources, Health Resources and Services Administration. (n.d.). *The National Survey of Children With Special Health Care Needs chartbook 2005–2006.* Retrieved November 11, 2008, from http://mchb.hrsa.gov/cshcn05

U.S. Public Health Service. (2001). *Report of the Surgeon General's conference on children's mental health: A national action agenda.* Washington, DC: Department of Health and Human Services.

Van den Hoofdakker, B. J. M., Van der Veen-mulders, L., Sytema, S., Emmelkamp, P. M., Ruud, N., & Maaike, H. (2007). Effectiveness of behavioral parent training for children with ADHD in routine clinical practice: A randomized controlled study. *Journal of the American Academy of Child & Adolescent Psychiatry, 46*, 1263–1271.

Waxmonsky, J. (2002, Oct.). *Donepezil (Aricept) may improve executive functioning in ADHD.* Presented at the 49th annual meeting of the American Academy of Child and Adolescent Psychiatry, San Francisco.

Weber, W., Vander Stoep, A., McCarty, R. L., Weiss, N. S., Biederman, J., & McClellan, J. (2008). Hypericum perforatum (St John's wort) for attention-deficit/hyperactivity disorder in children and adolescents: A randomized controlled trial. *Journal of the American Medical Association, 299*, 2633–2641

Weinfeld, R., Barnes-Robinson, L., Jeweler, S., & Roffman Shevitz, B. (2006). *Smart kids with learning difficulties: Overcoming obstacles and realizing potential.* Waco, TX: Prufrock Press.

Weinfeld, R., & Davis, M. (2008). *Special needs advocacy resource book.* Waco, TX: Prufrock Press.

Weiss, G., & Hechtman, L. T. (1993). Hyperactive children grown up (2nd ed.). New York: Guilford.

Weiss, M., Safren, S. A., Solanto, M. V., Hechtman, L., Rostain, A. L., Ramsay, J. R., et al. (2008). Research forum on psychological treatment of adults with ADHD. *Journal of Attention Disorders, 11,* 642–651.

Wilens, T. E., Hammerness, P., & Spencer, T. (2006, May). Combined OROS methylphenidate and atomoxetine treatment in children and adolescents with ADHD. Presented at the 159th Annual Meeting of the American Psychiatric Association, Toronto, Ontario, Canada.

WrightsLaw. (n.d.). *Joint policy memorandum (ADD).* Retrieved November 5, 2008, from http://www.wrightslaw.com/law/code_regs/OSEP_Memorandum_ADD_1991.html

Young, J. L., & Giwerc, D. (2003, Dec.). Just what is coaching? *Attention!,* 36–41.

Zubin, J. (1975). Problem of attention in schizophrenia. In M. L. Kietzman, S. Sutton, & J. Zubin (Eds.). Experimental approaches to psychopathology (pp. 139–166). New York: Academies Press.

Zylowska, S. L., Ackerman, D. L., Yang, M. H., Futrell, J. L., Horton, N. L., Hale, T. S., et al. (2008). Mindfulness meditation training in adults and adolescents with ADHD. *Journal of Attention Disorders, 11,* 737–746.

Appendix A

*Supplementary Tools for Use
With Individuals With ADHD*

Famous People With ADHD or Learning Disabilities

Knowing that you are not alone is helpful to many people. The following people have struggled with ADHD or learning disabilities and have made substantial contributions to society. They may be a source of inspiration and motivation.

- Bill Gates
- Michael Jordan
- Stephen Spielberg
- Frank Lloyd Wright
- Salvador Dali
- Pablo Picasso
- Vincent Van Gogh
- Terry Bradshaw
- Pete Rose
- Nolan Ryan
- Will Smith
- Charlotte Brönte
- Emily Brönte
- Samuel Clemens
- Emily Dickinson
- Edgar Allan Poe
- Ralph Waldo Emerson
- Robert Frost
- George Bernard Shaw
- Henry David Thoreau

- Leo Tolstoy
- Tennessee Williams
- Virginia Woolf
- William Butler Yeats
- Wolfgang Amadeus Mozart
- Andrew Carnegie
- Malcolm Forbes
- Henry Ford
- Stevie Wonder
- Paul Orfalea
- Ted Turner
- Christopher Columbus
- Meriwether Lewis
- Anne Bancroft
- Jim Carrey
- Cher
- Jack Nicholson
- Jimi Hendrix
- Dustin Hoffman
- Whoopi Goldberg

- Walt Disney
- Tom Cruise
- Henry Winkler
- Elvis Presley
- Evel Knievel
- Robbie Knievel
- William J. Clinton
- Danny Glover
- Carl Lewis
- Charles Schwab
- Galileo
- Jules Verne
- Sylvester Stallone
- Robin Williams
- Orville Wright
- Wilbur Wright
- Alexander Graham Bell
- Thomas Edison
- Benjamin Franklin
- Ansel Adams
- Albert Einstein
- James Carville
- John F. Kennedy
- Abraham Lincoln
- Admiral Richard Byrd

- Dwight D. Eisenhower
- Babe Ruth
- Leonardo Da Vinci
- William Randolph Hearst
- Diane Swonk
- Carl Jung
- Anwar Sadat
- Eleanor Roosevelt
- Gen. H. Norman Schwarzkopf
- Howard Hughes
- King Karl XI of Sweden
- Lindsay Wagner
- Lord Alfred Tennyson
- Lord Byron
- Louis Pasteur
- Luci Baines Johnson
- Magic Johnson
- Robert Frost
- Robert Kennedy
- Robert Louis Stevenson
- Socrates
- Stephen Hawking
- Thomas Jefferson
- Walt Whitman
- Michael Phelps

What Defines Me as a Successful Learner?

Who I Am! (Strengths and Needs)

_____

_____

_____

What I Need! (Adaptations and Accommodations)

_____

_____

_____

Which Tools Work For Me?
(Interventions and Strategies)

_____

_____

_____

How to Get What I Need to Succeed!

_____

_____

_____

Adaptations and Accommodations Checklist

Research has revealed that the principles put forth here are the best practices for providing appropriate adaptations and accommodations:

_____ Accommodations used in assessments should parallel accommodations that are integrated into classroom instruction.

_____ The adaptations/accommodations are aligned with the educational impact of the individual student's disability and the adaptations/accommodations are aligned with the needs described in the student's IEP or 504 plan.

_____ The adaptations/accommodations are based upon the strengths of the student.

_____ Accommodations are based on what students need in order to be provided with an equal opportunity to show what they know without impediment of their disability.

_____ Assessments allow students, while using appropriate accommodations, to demonstrate their skills without interference from their disabilities

_____ After selecting and providing appropriate adaptations/accommodations, their impact on the performance of the individual student is evaluated and only those that are effective are continued.

_____ The adaptations/accommodations are reviewed, revised, and when appropriate, faded over time, allowing the student to move from dependence to independence.

_____ A multidisciplinary team, which considers the input of the parent and student, decides upon the adaptations/accommodations.

_____ The appropriate adaptations/accommodations and the rationale for each of them are shared with all staff members who work with the student.

(*Note.* Adapted from *Smart Kids With Learning Difficulties: Overcoming Obstacles and Realizing Potential* (pp. 69–71), by R. Weinfeld, L. Barnes-Robinson, S. Jeweler, B. Roffman Shevitz, 2006, Waco, TX: Prufrock Press. Copyright© 2006, Prufrock Press. Adapted with permission.)

Sample Daily Home/School Report Card

Student's Name: _____

Date: _____

Circle one number for each behavior below.

Remains on task during class work   1   2   3   4   5

Raises hand to participate   1   2   3   4   5

Comes to class prepared   1   2   3   4   5

Comments:

_____

_____

_____

_____

_____

Note: 1 = very poor; 2 = poor; 3 = satisfactory; 4 = good; 5 = very good

Appendix B

Extended Information on Research of Attention Deficit Hyperactivity Disorder

Current Research Sources

Several reports release updated information about the current research initiatives related to ADHD so that individuals can keep abreast of the most recent and potentially helpful findings.

- The *Attention Research Update*, written by David Rabiner, Ph.D., a senior research scientist at Duke University, is a monthly report designed to help parents, professionals, and educators stay informed about new research on ADHD. The newsletter reviews promising new research on ADHD treatments, educational strategies for children with ADHD, how ADHD impacts development, and a variety of other issues. Free subscriptions to this newsletter are available through the following Web site: http://www.helpforadd.com.

- The *ADHD Report*, written by Russell Barkley, Ph.D., and other leading ADHD experts, discusses issues related to ADHD. It includes handouts for clinicians and parents and has annotated research findings. Annual subscriptions to the newsletter are available from Guilford Press at http://www.guilford.com. In the search box on the Guilford Press Web site enter "ADHD Report Barkley" to locate the *ADHD Report*.

Reading the literature and diligently accessing available resources are helpful strategies for obtaining the most current and accurate information related to ADHD.

The Multimodal Treatment Study (MTA): An Overview of the Importance of Multimodal Systems for ADHD

In Chapter 1, the authors refer to the pivotal, historically important, Multimodal Treatment Study (MTA) of Children with ADHD. To review, this was a randomized clinical trial of 579 children ages 7–9 years receiving 14 months of medication (MED), behavioral treatment (BEH), combined treatment (COMB: medication and behavioral treatment), and routine community care (CC). Intensive versions of state-of-the-art treatment approaches were compared. There were 19 measures of six variables: (a) ADHD symptoms, (b) aggression-oppositional defiant disorder, (c) internalizing symptoms, (d) social skills, (e) parent-child relations, and (f) academic achievement. It is important to note that although there were 579 subjects, each site had only 24 participants per treatment group.

There were four treatment groups at each of six sites in the United States and in Canada. All the children were diagnosed as experiencing ADHD, combined type. The three most common comorbid disorders were oppositional defiant disorder (39.9%), anxiety disorders (33.5%), and conduct disorder (14.3%). Approximately 61% of the children were White, 20% African-American, and 8% Hispanic. The educational levels of mothers and fathers were 94% and 90% high school educated, respectively. Income levels were balanced into 3 ranges. Household family composition was 69% two-parent households and 30% one-parent households.

The BEH group treatment consisted of parent training, school-based intervention, and a summer treatment program. Parent training in child behavior management or what is often referred to as parent management training (PMT), involved 27 group and 8 individual sessions. The school-based intervention included biweekly teacher consultation by the counselor on classroom behavior management (10–16 weeks), a classroom aide (12 weeks), and the use of a daily behavior report card. The teacher-completed report card focused on targeted behaviors and was brought home by the child for home-based rewards. The summer treatment program (8 weeks) involved use of a point system, time-out, social reinforcement, modeling, social-skills training, group problem solving, and sports-skills training. PMT was the only BEH intervention that was used during the last few months of the study, occurring approximately once per month.

The MED group consisted of intensive and closely monitored medication management starting with a double-blind, placebo-controlled trial of methylphenidate (MPH; Ritalin) three times daily over 28 days. Each child in this group received all administered medication conditions in a random fashion (placebo, 5mg., 10mg., 15mg. or 20mg.). After the medication trial, the optimal dose was then used throughout the study with close monitoring. If the child did not benefit from MPH, then a protocol of alternative medications was implemented until an appropriate medication was found. Compared to the BEH group, MED treatment occurred every day for 14 months.

The COMB group received both BEH and MED treatments for 14 months. The CC group was referred to community mental health resources. Hence, this group did not receive any of the intensive treatment approaches but approximately 67% of the children in this group received medications, as per their usual treatment.

For ADHD symptoms, careful medication management (maintained through 14 months) was superior to BEH alone (faded by 14 months) and to routine CC that included medication. Although COMB showed significant advantages over CC in every domain (whereas MEDMGT did not), it did not prove significantly superior to MEDMGT for individual specific outcome measures. However, COMB did show modest significant advantages over MEDMGT on global or composite outcome indices. COMB also provided modestly greater benefits than MEDMGT for non-ADHD symptom domains and positive functioning, as well as greater levels of parent satisfaction. This additive effect was more pronounced for children with two comorbidities, that is, those with both internalizing mood disorders (depression and/or anxiety disorder) and disruptive behavior disorders (conduct or oppositional defiant disorder).

Many have debated the strengths and weaknesses of the MTA study. Greene and Ablon (2001) argued for greater attention to cognitive behavioral methods of treatment and more tailored multimodal interventions. Abikoff (2001) and Hoza (2001) clarified and defended some of the decisions made in the design of the study, stating, for example that cognitive-behavioral treatments did not have a proven history with children. They also conceded to some of the limitations of the study. Conners, Epstein, and March (2001) conducted a reanalysis of the MTA data, revealing that the COMB group was statistically superior to all the other groups including the MED group, suggesting that the COMB treatment approach is promising.

Still, if the results of the MTA study are true, and we know that medication is a most powerful aide for ADHD, why do we need a multimodal system? Although conclusions from the MTA study prove that the use of stimulants alone was more effective than behavioral and other therapies in controlling the core symptoms of ADHD inattention, hyperactivity/impulsiveness, and aggression, for other areas of functioning, such as anxiety symptoms, academic performance, and social skills, the combination of stimulant use with intensive behavioral therapies was consistently more effective. In addition, families and teachers reported higher levels of satisfaction for treatments that included behavioral therapy components.

Roughly 20% to 30% of children do not react favorably to stimulant medication. In children who do respond, the reaction to medication alone often is not sufficient to bring their academic performance into the typical range (Weiss & Hechtman, 1993). Moreover, despite some evidence for short-term academic gains, it is not clear if beneficial treatment effects are maintained when psychostimulant medication is used as a long-term treatment for academic functioning (Pelham & Murphy, 1986; Swanson, McBurnett, & Wigal, 1993). Finally, even when medication appears to be promising for controlling the behaviors that negatively affect the academic functioning of children with ADHD, educators have little control over who receives medication. Given these significant limitations, the identification and development of effective nonmedical interventions that enhance the academic functioning of children with ADHD is necessary.

In general, kids with ADHD are not able to monitor and control their behavior on their own. Consistency and support from concerned adults provides a feeling of safety and order through the knowledge that behavior has the same or similar expectations and consequences in all environments. Consistent support helps to reinforce effective behaviors for executive functioning and participation in school and community life.

There may not be agreement or adequate research at this time to demonstrate what percentage each component contributes to the effectiveness of a treatment plan as a whole. There is no single decision tree that shows parents, educators, and clinicians "if this works or doesn't work, then go to the next step." But, a rich tapestry of supports certainly employs contemporary elements of best practices in child-rearing and education that may increase effective functioning and quality of life for children who otherwise would feel defeated by their inability to sustain attention and effort in meeting the complex demands of our modern world.

A multimodal treatment plan is especially important for hyperactive/impulsive and combined types with inattention, where research demonstrates that such a plan is more frequently required. Hazelwood et al. (2002) concluded that multimodal approaches are found to be effective by practitioners, especially when there are coexisting conditions, but there was no universal agreement as to what multimodal plans consist of. Thus, there needs to be a number of elements available for a tailor-made program for any given child (or adult) receiving treatment. No single intervention has emerged as maximally effective across all symptoms and domains. Use of a multimodal plan is just as much a prescriptive clinical art as it is a science alone. It involves trained and experienced clinical judgment.

In the absence of a plan, negative behavior seems to spring like weeds through cracks in concrete sidewalks. It can't be ignored. Mostly unwittingly, children with both ADHD and behavior problems find ways to frustrate adults, because adults rarely have a consistent management plan. As Goldstein (2000) points out, the behavior of children with ADHD quickly regresses when management strategies are absent.

The following is a brief summary of the practice guidelines from the American Academy of Pediatrics (2001). After an accurate diagnosis, the following is recommended for the treatment of a child diagnosed with ADHD:

- Primary care clinicians should establish a treatment program that recognizes ADHD as a chronic condition.

- The treating clinician, parents, and child, in collaboration with school personnel, should specify appropriate target outcomes to guide management.

- The clinician should recommend stimulant medication and/or behavior therapy as appropriate to improve target outcomes in children with ADHD. (Since the time of publication of these guidelines, a variety of nonstimulant medications have been approved and employed.)

- When the selected management for a child with ADHD has not met target outcomes, clinicians should evaluate the original diagnosis, use of all appropriate treatments, adherence to the treatment plan, and presence of coexisting conditions.

- The clinician should periodically provide a systematic follow-up for the child with ADHD. Monitoring should be directed to target outcomes and adverse effects, with information gathered from parents, teachers, and the child. (p. 1036)

In light of the high prevalence of ADHD in pediatric practice, the guidelines were intended for use by primary care clinicians for the management of children between 6 and 12 years of age with ADHD. Although many of the recommendations also applied to children with coexisting conditions, they primarily addressed children with ADHD, but without major coexisting conditions. Wisely, the guidelines were not intended as a sole source of rules for the treatment of children with

ADHD. The AAP report stated that the guidelines are "not intended to replace clinical judgment or to establish a protocol for all children with this condition, and may not provide the only appropriate approach to this problem" (p. 1033). They realized that, as a chronic condition, the family and child require information about the condition, and that knowledge needed updating, as research became more revealing. Families needed demystification. The authors understood that counseling might be required to help families adjust to the condition. They realized that primary care providers needed to be available to provide information and to help families set appropriate goals. They saw that children with ADHD required child-specific plans with monitoring and follow-up. Finally, the authors concluded, "The long-term care of a child with ADHD requires an ongoing partnership among clinicians, parents, teachers, and the child" and also recommended the input of other school personnel such as nurses and counselors (p. 1036).

Despite the frequently stated official guidelines from organizations like the American Academy of Pediatrics, there continue to be very single-pointed and oversimplified treatment plans often based on medication alone, when more services are required.

The Diagnostic Assessment of ADHD

The purpose of obtaining a diagnosis is to be able to establish that reported symptoms meet specific criteria, such as in the DSM system. If so, the clinician knows that the individual may be dealing with a life-long or, at least, a developmentally protracted condition that will require monitoring and treatment over a number of years. The persistence of the disorder must be accounted for and considered as a long-term challenge.

This section of Appendix B focuses on the diagnostic assessment process. The authors recognize the technical nature of some of the information discussed in this section. Therefore, Chapter 4 is intended to specifically address in a more concrete and accessible manner the role that parents are able to assume in finding the appropriate clinician to complete the assessment, contributing during the evaluation, and advocating for their child following the diagnosis.

Complexities in the Diagnosis

Children differ in the severity and number of symptoms of ADHD. Unlike a number of health conditions, there is no one, single test for ADHD (and that would be assuming that ADHD is a single unitary entity). Its varieties may not have one consistent cause. In each particular individual, one or more symptoms may manifest more strongly than others. Some children will be more impulsive and others more restless or inattentive. There are variations in the breadth of situations in which the primary symptoms are manifested and in the frequency and intensity of occurrence. It is true, however, that a person with ADHD will generally conform to the DSM requirement by displaying the pivotal behaviors across multiple environments.

As was mentioned in Chapter 1, it is very important to rule out ADHD look-alikes or temporary conditions that are characterized by inattention or restlessness. Ruling out competing diagnoses is called *differential diagnosis.* Increasingly, preliminary medical examinations are found to be a best practice where feasible.

There are complexities in the DSM-IV diagnosis. The DSM-IV criteria hinge on behavior "inconsistent with developmental level." Although the symptoms are generally seen much before age 7, the diagnosis for ADHD can be made in adulthood, but the history generally reflects symptoms in childhood.

The future looks increasingly bright with respect to more and more precise neuro-imaging studies and the identification of genetic makers and combinations of genes. At the present time, however, the proper formation of the diagnosis pivots on the trained skills of a clinician who integrates data from many sources of information. This procedure can result in a working decision that ADHD is in fact present, that the manifestation in a given person can be reliably described, and that the condition has practical effects in everyday living. The diagnostic procedure requires a highly trained professional, usually a licensed or certified psychologist, school psychologist, psychiatrist, or properly trained pediatrician. All too often, practitioners have been relying on only one or two methods to confirm the diagnosis. However, Demaray, Schaefer, and DeLong (2003) conducted a national survey of training and assessment practices in the schools. The results confirmed a substantial caseload of ADHD referrals in schools, as is found in clinics. In the assessment of ADHD, the results indicated that school psychologists are using multiple informants, methods, and settings, with rating scales, observations, and interviews the most common methods identified.

Components of the Assessment Battery

Some cases presented to the clinician are simple and straightforward. The history meets with early diagnostic markers. The child presents with simple, consistent, symptoms. Parent and school observations overlap. In cases like this, where all indications are very clear, an assessment battery may not be necessary. A treatment plan, including consideration of medication, can be put into place.

In cases that are unclear or more complex, the follow components are recommended:

1. a thorough medical and developmental history,

2. one or more observations in a natural environment such as home or school,

3. rating scales from multiple environments and observers,

4. psychometric instruments,

5. Continuous Performance Tests (CPT), and

6. an interview with the child.

A Thorough Medical and Developmental History

This component refers to a review of available records and an interview with the parent(s) or guardian(s). There are a number of structured and unstructured history formats, published and unpublished. Some histories have questions directly linked to the DSM criteria for ADHD or for a number of conditions. Some formats are designed for ADHD clinics and some for clinic intake processes in general. Structured interviews, where the same questions are asked of each participant, can be used normatively to compare children (Anastopoulos & Barkley, 1992). Unstructured interviews are flexible. They can seem more human in addressing the concerns of the interviewee and they can provide more anecdotal data. However, they are more likely to be unreliable in diagnosis (Schaughency & Rothlind, 1991). Hinshaw (1994) has held that a thorough developmental and family history might provide the most information.

One or More Observations in a Natural Environment

The observation may be informal and unstructured or based on some repeatable format. Diagnosis optimally is based on direct observation (Barkley, 1998). There are a number of structured observation formats, such as time sampling, in which the child's behavior is described at various intervals. Researchers often have criticized the use of waiting room behaviors by doctors in making the diagnosis, but Edwards et al. (2005) showed that ratings from unstructured clinical observations correlated significantly with ratings made by parents (but not by teachers). These findings were for the hyperactive/impulsive type and not for the inattentive type.

Rating Scales From Multiple Environments and Observers

Examples of rating scale systems include measures like the Conners' Rating Scales-Revised (Conners, 1997), or the ADHD–IV rating scales by DuPaul, Power, Anastopoulous, and Reid (1998). Generally, due to the frequency of coexisting executive functioning problems, a measure like the Behavior Rating Inventory of Executive Function (BRIEF; Gioia et al., 2000) should be included. The BRIEF attempts to measure the ability to inhibit, shift, emotionally control, regulate behavior, initiate tasks, utilize working memory, plan, organize, and monitor behavior. Rating scales should be administered to one or both parents or guardians, one or more teachers or staff members familiar with the child at school, and, when possible, to the person being rated. Many rating scales, like the Conners system, include self-report measures. Also, there are some rating scales that are "omnibus" tests, which measure a wide range of child and adolescent psychopathology, such as the Behavior Assessment System for Children–2 (BASC-2; Reynolds & Kamphaus, 2004). It is important to note that rating scales have been found to be generally valid and reliable in large samples, but in many individual cases, they are subject to the personal biases of the rater. It is not unusual for parent and teacher ratings to differ significantly and there can be differences in perceptions between two teachers in the same school. The rater should be carefully instructed to base ratings on the subject's actual behavior with which they are familiar, and not what they imagine or hope it to be in a given situation. In addition to diagnosis, rating scales frequently are used to monitor the effectiveness of medication and other treatments (Barkley, 1990).

Psychometric Instruments

There is an important difference in the science of behavioral measurement between face validity and statistical validity. Face validity refers to tests and measures that appear to make sense and to be appropriate ways of predicting behavior. Statistical validity requires proof. Many tests look and feel like they should be measuring something important when, in fact, they add little or nothing. Rapport, Chung, Shore, Denney, and Isaacs (2000) identified 142 studies published between 1980 and 1999 that compared the performance of children with ADHD and normal controls on neurocognitive tests and experimentally designed studies. They labeled instruments "reliable" if they were studied by at least three independent investigators that yielded significant differences between ADHD and control groups in at least 75% of the studies. Unreliable instruments were those that showed differences between groups in 25% of the studies or less (Rapport et al.). Reliable tasks tended to be those that required a timed "speeded" response and that relied on working memory, especially those tasks that placed demands on subvocal speech or the use of talking to one's self internally to hold information in working memory during the task. With only one exception (Wechsler Coding), all of the reliable tests also involved not having the response stimulus continuously present, thus requiring working memory. That is, the child was required to identify, match, or recognize something previously exposed (albeit only a second or a few seconds before). Finally, tests were more reliable if the pacing of the presentation of test items was controlled by an adult administering the test and not self-paced by the child (Rapport et al.).

Continuous Performance Tests (CPT)

In Continuous Performance Tests (CPT) subjects are instructed to respond to numbers, letters, or the differences between geometric forms by pressing a button or computer space bar when they see a target they have been trained to detect and refrain from responding to a stimulus that differs in some preidentified way from the target. Performance measures may include correct responses, errors of omission (not responding to a target), errors of commission (responding when the target is not present), and reaction times. The value of the inclusion of a continuous performance testing in the assessment battery has been the subject of debate.

Edwards et al. (2007) evaluated the validity and classification utility of the Conners' Continuous Performance Test II, Version 5 (CCPT-II) in the assessment of inattentive, hyperactive-impulsive behaviors in children. They found no significant positive correlations between the CCPT parameters and parent and teacher ratings of inattention and hyperactive-impulsive behaviors. Although the CCPT was not accurate in discriminating ADHD from control subjects, it was slightly more accurate when identifying problem with hyperactive-impulsive behaviors.

Turkelson, Goldstein, Doggett, Mitchell, and Tregear (2000) did not find clear specificity in predicting real-world ADHD symptoms from CPTs and were unable to find literature that supported or did not support CPTs for monitoring medication effects. Published reports of national professional medical associations, national medical policy organization positions, or reports of national expert opinion organizations did not demonstrate a consensus in the medical community that CPTs were safe and efficacious for the purpose of making the ADHD diagnosis. All guidelines advised against the use of CPTs alone (Turkelson et al., 2000).

Despite these negative findings, researchers have been working to further refine the accuracy and relevancy of such measures. Rubia (2002) successfully compared normal controls with children with ADHD on a task battery, measuring cognitive control, motor inhibition, cognitive inhibition, sustained attention, and time discrimination. The children with ADHD showed an inconsistent and premature response style across all six tasks presented. Rubia describes the relationship to a general description of impulsivity as an "inappropriately speedy, premature, highly changeable, and non-persistent, poorly controlled, unreflective, and immediacy-bound response style" (p. 47) that affects predominantly the output level of behavior. An important finding of this study was the inconsistency with which children with ADHD respond across tasks. Also, although ADHD has been thought to have a volitional or motivational component, Rubia was unable to influence accuracy with rewards. This demonstrates that, for children with ADHD, the symptoms are not fully under the control of the child.

There has been debate over the utility of tests that involve real-world assessments in natural or clinical environments and in testing with laboratory equipment in the psychologist's office, such as CPTs.

Interview With the Child

Although potentially unreliable, no one knows how it feels to experience ADHD better than the person who "has" the disorder. Many children can describe the frustration they feel in needing directions repeated in school, experiencing the embarrassment of peer rejection, the aggravation of losing things, the inability to sit still, and the need to read things over and over to comprehend. Many children are amazed at experiencing for the first time that someone cares about how they experience their ability to control their attention or external behavior. In developing a management plan, the chances of success are multiplied significantly by having the child "on board" with his or her own treatment. By creating a working relationship with the child during the initial interview, there is an increased likelihood of compliance and, therefore, successful treatment.

Should an IQ Test Be Administered in Identifying ADHD?

It is inappropriate to test children with too many or unnecessary instruments. A trained professional assembles a comprehensive test battery on only what is needed. Given the precaution to protect children from unnecessary assessment, it is unnecessary and unwise to administer an IQ test in some cases. On the other hand, when important information is sought about a number of areas of functioning, an IQ test may be very valuable in helping to identify areas of strength and weaknesses for planning purposes.

The effects of intelligence on measures of ADHD have been noted in several studies. It often is assumed that brighter students can control some test results on continuous performance tests and psychometric tests. Naglieri, Goldstein, Delauder, and Schwebach (2005) explored the relationships between the Wechsler Intelligence Scale for Children Third Edition (WISC-III) and the Cognitive Assessment System with Conners' rating scales and continuous performance tests: 117 children aged 6–16 years who were referred to a specialty clinic were evaluated who had a primary (45%) or secondary (36%) diagnosis of ADHD. All children were given the WISC-III, Cognitive Assessment System (CAS), the CPT, and Conners' Parent and Teacher Rating Scales—Revised, Long Form. Correlations between Conners' Behavior Rating Scale and Conners' Continuous Performance Test were uniformly low and nonsignificant (the highest correlation was .17). Correlations between the WISC-III and Conners' Parent Rating

Scale were all nonsignificant, but teacher ratings showed significant correlations between most of the WISC-III factors and the Cognitive Problems/Inattention scores. Few significant correlations were found between CPT with the WISC-III and CAS. These results suggest that practitioners should expect to find a lack of consistency between the scores provided by these two kinds of tests. This demonstrates the importance of clinical judgment in integrating test information, where different kinds of measures are combined. Children with ADHD earn average scores on all measures of the CAS except they tend to receive lower scores in Planning (Naglieri, Goldstein, Iseman, & Schwebach, 2003). Therefore, the CAS appears sensitive to the cognitive processing difficulties in Planning experienced by children with ADHD and assists in differentiating children with ADHD from children with other psychological disorders.

According to a survey of school psychologists, intelligence tests such as the Wechsler Intelligence Scale for Children frequently are used in the diagnosis of ADHD (Pfeiffer, Reddy, Kletzel, Schmelzer, & Boyer, 2000). Barkley (1998) stated that no subtest or configuration of subtests in the Wechsler scales is sensitive or specific to ADHD. He stated that ADHD results from a failure in self-control. However, he stated that no aspect of the Wechsler scale, including the Freedom From Distractibility factor, which was frequently used by professionals to identify ADHD in earlier versions of the test, measures behavioral inhibition. He concluded that this measure does not accurately identify children with ADHD and it was dropped in the WISC-IV.

Early Diagnostic Identification of ADHD in the Preschool Child

In 2007, Smith and Corkum published a review of measures used to diagnose preschool-aged children with ADHD. They noted that the diagnosis of ADHD in preschool children is challenging because the behaviors exhibited in ADHD are not uncommon for many children this age. Therefore, assessing preschoolers needs to be multifaceted and requires the use of a variety of assessment techniques. They categorized the assessment measures used to identify ADHD in preschoolers into four core areas: standardized rating scales, structured interviews, direct observations of behavior, and direct measures of attention and hyper-activity-impulsivity. The authors noted that their review might not have highlighted some measures used in clinical practice. The authors found the diagnosis of ADHD in preschoolers to be difficult.

Although a number of rating scales exist to assess behaviors associated with ADHD in preschool children, there are comparatively fewer structured interviews, developmentally appropriate structured behavior observation measures, and direct measures of early attention and hyperactivity-impulsivity. Smith and Corkum (2007) note that understanding whether a child's symptoms persist beyond what may be expected for typical development or what may be encountered in a stressful situation is essential to the diagnosis of ADHD. The early identification of ADHD in preschool children is both a possible danger and a possible blessing. There is the chance of overidentification of behaviors that are characteristic of a young child as pathological, such as playfulness, exploratory behavior, high activity, and normal spontaneity. The positive outcome of accurate early identification is to prevent the onset of negative experiences of peer rejection, school ejection, and low self-esteem.

About the
Authors

Stephan M. Silverman, Ph.D., retired in July 2008 after 30 years as a school psychologist in the Montgomery County Public Schools in Montgomery County, MD (MCPS). He has maintained a private practice since 1975. Silverman specializes in the diagnosis, treatment, and instruction of children, adolescents, and adults with attention deficits, learning disabilities, and low incidence developmental disorders, including autistic spectrum disorders. He specializes in working with parents of children with disabilities and children who underachieve and evaluates and counsels young adults with disabilities in life transitions. He has lectured nationally to a wide group of psychologists, educators, and related health providers on topics such as learning disabilities, ADHD, and Asperger's syndrome. Silverman worked in a private research group investigating combat stress in American helicopter pilots during the Vietnam conflict. He also served as a child psychologist in a developmental assessment clinic in Israel in the early 1970s. Silverman is the coauthor of the best-selling *School Success for Kids With Asperger's Syndrome* with Richard Weinfeld, also published by Prufrock Press.

Jacqueline S. Iseman, Ph.D., is a licensed psychologist with a private practice in Potomac, MD. She received her bachelor's degree from Cornell University, and her Ph.D. in Clinical Psychology from George Mason University. She has worked in a variety of hospital, school, and clinic settings including Children's National Medical Center in Washington, DC, the Devereux Foundation's Day School in Pennsylvania, and several private practices in Maryland and Virginia. Iseman's research on differential diagnosis of ADHD was published in the article "Performance of Children with Attention Deficit Hyperactivity Disorder and Anxiety/Depression on the WISC-III and Cognitive Assessment System (CAS)." In Iseman's private practice, Hands on Health Psychological Services, LLC (http://www.handsonpsychology.com), she provides support and guidance to her clients in order to provide pathways toward developing healthier and more fulfilling lives. Her areas of expertise include working with children, adolescents, and families providing psychotherapy, consultations, and assessment. Iseman enjoys treating clients with a broad range of psychological concerns. Her approach is practical and comprehensive, addressing each individual's issues within the context of the family, school, and community.

Sue Jeweler, a retired teacher, spent her 30-year career in Maryland's Montgomery County Public Schools. Jeweler has been a consultant to the John F. Kennedy Center for the Performing Arts, the Smithsonian Institution, National Geographic, Berns & Kay, and Street Law. Her expertise has been used in a variety of projects with an outreach to teachers nationally and internationally. She has coauthored two educational kits, numerous journal articles, and more than 40 books including the best-selling *Smart Kids With Learning Difficulties: Overcoming Obstacles and Realizing Potential*. Jeweler, an award-winning educator, is the recipient of the prestigious *Washington Post* Agnes Meyer Outstanding Teaching Award. She is listed in *Who's Who Among America's Teachers*, *Who's Who of American Women*, and the *International Who's Who*. She coestablished Creative Family Projects, LLC, which identifies problems and provides solutions by synthesizing information from organizations, institutions, and corporations into booklets and training modules for the benefit of children, youth, and families. Jeweler is married with children and has one grandchild.

About the
Contributors

Lance D. Clawson, M.D., F.A.A.C.A.P.,
graduated with honors from the University of
Southern California and Tufts University School of
Medicine. He is a Fellow of the American Academy
of Child and Adolescent Psychiatry. He received his
postdoctoral training in general psychiatry and child
and adolescent psychiatry at Walter Reed Army
Medical Center in Washington, DC. After completing his postgraduate training, Clawson served
as the Chief of Child & Adolescent Psychiatry and
then the Chief of Psychiatry for the U.S. Armed
Forces in the Republic of Korea. After leaving the
Army, he served as medical director at the Division
of Child & Adolescent Psychiatry at the University
of Maryland at Baltimore School of Medicine. He
currently is in private practice in Cabin John, MD.
Clawson has published on such topics as the mental
health needs of homeless children, mental health
consultation in schools, working effectively with

pediatricians, play therapy, and developing clinical databases for mental health systems of care.

Shoshana Silverman Belisle, LMSW, earned her bachelor's degree at the University of North Carolina at Chapel Hill and her master's degree in social work at New York University. She is a licensed master social worker in New York, and also is certified in Ericksonian Hypnotherapy. Shoshana has held a number of roles at the Continuum Center for Health and Healing, a division of Beth Israel Medical Center and a leader in integrative medicine, which combines conventional medicine with alternative, complementary, and indigenous healing approaches. She has coordinated and helped publish research studies in integrative medicine, developed a psychotherapy practice as part of the Center's Mind-Body Program, and most recently, furthered the Center's marketing and fundraising efforts, focusing on expanding the Center's holistic initiatives for inpatients and hospital staff through Beth Israel's new Department of Integrative Medicine. In her own life, she incorporates nutrition, meditation, exercise, yoga, and an ongoing exploration of new avenues to promote wellness in body, mind, and spirit.

Jennifer Engel Fisher, M.ED, is the Assistant Director of Weinfeld Education Group, LLC, an educational consulting group located in Silver Spring, MD. Jennifer earned her bachelor's degree from the University of Maryland, Baltimore County, and her master's degree in Special Education from Johns Hopkins University. Jennifer has been a special educator in both inclusion and self-contained classrooms that served a variety of populations including persons with ADHD, LD, Asperger's syndrome, and students with emotional disturbance. Jennifer serves as an advocate for students in elementary through high school and conducts organizational coaching for students, especially those with executive functioning difficulties. Jennifer lives with her husband and two children outside Washington, DC.